AMAZING NEW YORK!

FALL IN LOVE WITH NYC AND NEW YORK STATE THROUGH INTERESTING FUN FACTS AND FANTASTIC STORIES FOR THE ENTIRE FAMILY

AMAZING STATES OF AMERICA

MARIANNE JENNINGS

DISCLAIMER

Reader discretion is advised.

The author is not responsible for any sudden urges to develop thoughtful opinions about pizza, bagels, regional grocery stores, or whether something is truly "upstate."

Reading this book will not grant you the ability to navigate New York City sidewalks with expert confidence, master subway balance on your first ride, or predict lake-effect snow in Western New York with perfect accuracy. It may, however, make you more aware of how differently life moves across New York State—from the busiest city blocks to the quietest small towns.

While every effort has been made to ensure accuracy, the author bears no responsibility for readers who enthusiastically debate regional foods, give directions using landmarks that no longer exist, or discover that New York City is only one part of a much larger and wonderfully varied state.

Always remember: New York State is vast, diverse, and full of stories—and New York City is just one (very influential) piece of the puzzle.

For New Yorkers:
past, present, and adopted

CONTENTS

BONUS EBOOK

As a **special bonus** and as a **thank you** for purchasing this book, I created a **FREE New York companion quiz e-book** with **over 100 fun questions and answers** taken from this book.

Get the FREE bonus quiz e-book here:
https://tinyurl.com/nyquizbook-bonus

Test your knowledge of New York and quiz your friends.
Enjoy!

INTRODUCTION

So, you think you know New York?

This book explores **both New York City and New York State**, because the Empire State is far more than a single skyline or a single story. It's a place where roaring waterfalls and silent forests exist alongside tiny towns and one of the largest cities in the world—all shaped by geography, history, and everyday habits.

Did you know that New York has one of the largest state park systems in the country? That parts of the state still contain rare old-growth forests? Or that New York quietly played a role in everything from food innovations to Cold War defense? These are just a few examples of the fascinating facts hiding in plain sight.

In this book, you'll explore the quirky, surprising, and often unexpected facts that define life across New York—from the everyday behaviors that confuse visitors to the unusual history beneath familiar streets. You'll learn why certain foods inspire fierce loyalty, how geography shaped culture in dramatically different ways, and how New York's influence stretches far beyond its borders.

This isn't a travel guide. You won't find itineraries or "top ten" lists here. Instead, this book is packed with fact-checked, bite-sized fun facts, along with the context that explains why they matter.

Whether you're navigating busy city sidewalks, driving quiet upstate roads, or simply curious about how one state can contain so many different worlds, this book invites you to see New York—both the city and the state—in a whole new way.

Enjoy!
 - Marianne

INTRODUCTION TO THE EMPIRE STATE

Before we dive into pizza slices, skyscrapers, and snowstorms, let's set the stage. New York is more than a place—it's a symbol. From Indigenous nations and colonial history to state symbols and iconic slogans, the Empire State has always stood out. Here's a quick tour of New York's origins, borders, and bold spirit.

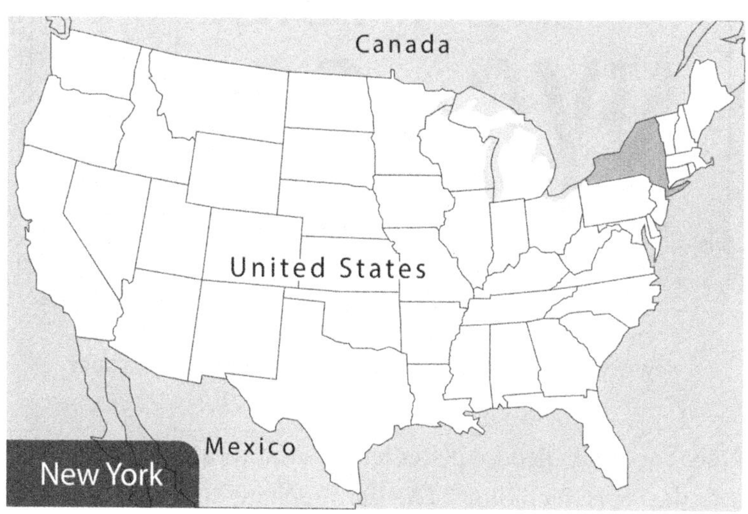

NEW YORK'S NAME AND WHAT IT MEANS

In 1664, the English seized the Dutch colony of New Netherland and renamed it New York to honor the Duke of York (later King James II of England). The Dutch had previously established the settlement of New Amsterdam, which became New York City under English control.

NEW YORK STATE'S NICKNAME

New York State is famously known as the "Empire State." This nickname is believed to have originated from a 1785 letter by George Washington, referring to New York as "the Seat of the Empire," highlighting its prominence and potential.

SLOGAN ON LICENSE PLATES

New York State license plate. Image via depositphotos.com

New York State license plates have featured various slogans over the years, including "The Empire State" and "I ♥ NY." In 2020, a new design was introduced that featured the state motto "Excelsior," along with images of landmarks such as Niagara Falls and the Statue of Liberty.

THE STATE MOTTO

New York's state motto is "Excelsior," which is Latin for "Ever Upward." This aspirational motto was adopted in 1778 and reflects New York's continuing ambition and forward-looking and the dramatic landscapes that inspired the Hudson River School of painting.

- **Capital District:** Centered around Albany, this region includes the cities of Troy, Schenectady, and Saratoga Springs, combining government functions with tech industry growth and cultural institutions.

- **Adirondacks:** This vast wilderness area covers 6 million acres in northern New York. The Adirondack Park is not a national or state park, but the area is larger than the national parks of Yellowstone, Yosemite, Grand Canyon, Glacier, and Olympic combined. The region is protected by New York State laws that preserve its forests and regulate development, and it includes a mix of public wilderness and privately owned land.

- **North Country:** The northernmost part of the state bordering Canada includes the Thousand Islands region along the St. Lawrence River and the Tug Hill Plateau, known for receiving the heaviest snowfall in the eastern U.S.

- **Central New York:** Home to Syracuse and numerous smaller cities, this region features the Finger Lakes, known for their wineries, scenic beauty, and outdoor recreation opportunities.

- **Southern Tier:** A region running along New York's border with Pennsylvania. It includes cities such as Binghamton, Elmira, and Corning, blending rural landscapes with industrial heritage and college towns.

- **Western New York:** Anchored by Buffalo, this region borders Lakes Erie and Ontario and includes Niagara Falls. It's known for its industrial heritage, distinct cuisine, and fierce winters.

DID YOU KNOW?

Much of the Adirondack Forest Preserve is protected by the New York State Constitution, which requires that state-owned forest lands be kept "**forever wild.**" That means the land cannot be sold, logged, or developed, helping preserve one of the largest wilderness areas in the eastern United States.

NEW YORK STATE FLAG

New York State Flag. Image via depositphotos.com

The New York State flag features the state coat of arms on a blue background. The coat of arms, adopted in 1778, depicts two figures: Liberty (with a revolutionary cap on a pole) and Justice (blindfolded, holding scales). Between them is a shield showing the Hudson River, with a smiling sun rising over mountains. Above this, an eagle is perched atop a globe. The banner below reads "Excelsior."

STATE SEAL

The Great Seal of New York features the state coat of arms. It has remained largely unchanged since 1778, making it one of the oldest continuously used state seals in America. The seal is used to authenticate official documents and is displayed in the New York State Capitol building in Albany.

NEW YORK STATE SYMBOLS

New York's state symbols include:

- **State Tree:** Sugar Maple
- **State Flower:** Rose
- **State Gem:** Garnet
- **State Shell:** Bay Scallop
- **State Animal:** Beaver
- **State Bird:** Eastern Bluebird
- **State Freshwater Fish:** Brook Trout
- **State Saltwater Fish:** Striped Bass
- **State Beverage:** Milk
- **State Fruit:** Apple
- **State Muffin:** Apple Muffin
- **State Insect:** Nine-Spotted Ladybug

STATE SONG

"I Love New York" is the official state song of New York, adopted in 1980. Composed by Steve Karmen, the song originated as part of a tourism campaign that also produced the iconic "I ♥ NY" logo designed by Milton Glaser.

The campaign was developed during a time when New York

City was facing financial difficulties, and it aimed to boost tourism and improve the state's image.

Lyrics to "I Love New York":

> *I Love New York,*
> *I Love New York,*
> *There isn't another like it.*
> *No matter where you go.*
> *And nobody can compare it.*
> *It's win, place, and show.*
> *New York is special.*
> *New York is different 'cause there's no place else*
> *on earth quite like New York and that's why I*
> > *Love New York.*

2

THE BIG APPLE

FUN FACTS ABOUT NEW YORK CITY

New York State is packed with history, scenery, and character, but nothing compares to the energy of New York City. Known as "The Big Apple," this world-famous metropolis is home to iconic landmarks, diverse neighborhoods, and unforgettable experiences.

This chapter celebrates the city that never sleeps—from its five bustling boroughs to its subway secrets and quirky traditions.

NYC'S MANY NICKNAMES: MORE THAN JUST THE BIG APPLE

New York City has picked up quite a few nicknames over the years—each one capturing a different slice of its personality, history, or reputation:

- **The Big Apple** – The nickname "Big Apple" was first used in the 1920s by New York City sportswriter John J. Fitz Gerald while covering horse racing. Jockeys referred to racing in New York as "the big apple" because the city's tracks offered the largest purses and the most prestigious races. Jazz musicians later adopted the phrase to describe playing in New York's top clubs—"the big time"—helping cement the nickname as one of the city's most famous.

- **The City That Never Sleeps** – A nickname that reflects New York's round-the-clock energy. From late-night Broadway shows and 24-hour diners to an always-buzzing subway system, NYC is famous for being alive at all hours.
- **Gotham** – Coined in 1807 by author Washington Irving to mock the city's politics, the name originally came from an old English village of "wise fools." It was later immortalized as Batman's gritty hometown, adding a layer of moody, urban cool.
- **The Empire City** – A nod to New York State's nickname, "The Empire State." This title emphasizes the city's influence and ambition as a powerhouse of industry, culture, and finance.
- **The Capital of the World** – A phrase often used to reflect NYC's global status. With the United Nations headquarters, Wall Street, and world-famous cultural institutions, many see it as a center for international diplomacy, money, and media.
- **More Than a Melting Pot** – For generations, New York City has been called a "melting pot," symbolizing cultures blending together. Today, some describe it as more of a "tossed salad" or "cultural mosaic," where communities maintain their languages, traditions, and identities while contributing to the whole. With over 180 languages spoken, NYC is one of the most linguistically diverse places on Earth.

PEOPLE, POPULATION, AND VISITORS

Over 8.4 million people live in New York City. That's almost half of New York State's total population packed into just 1% of its land area.

New York City is the most populous city in the United States, and if it were its own country, it would have more people than nations such as Austria, Israel, or Switzerland.

By comparison, here are the populations of some of the world's largest metropolitan areas:

- Tokyo — about 37 million
- Delhi — over 34.6 million
- São Paulo — about 22 million
- Paris — about 11.3 million
- London — about 9.8 million
- Los Angeles — about 13 million in the greater metropolitan area

A TOURIST TSUNAMI

Each year, over 65 million tourists visit NYC, coming to see iconic sights like Times Square, Central Park, and the Statue of Liberty. Tourism generates tens of billions in revenue annually.

Times Square alone sees over 330,000 pedestrians every day, and on major holidays, that number can top 1 million.

THE FIVE BOROUGHS: MINI CITIES WITHIN A CITY

Map of NYCs Five boroughs via depositphotos.com

New York City is made up of five boroughs, each with its own distinct character, history, and fun facts. Whether it's the towering skyscrapers of Manhattan, the diverse communities of Queens, or the cultural legacy of the Bronx, every borough has something special to offer.

Each borough's population:

- **Brooklyn:** ~2.7 million
- **Queens:** ~2.3 million
- **Manhattan:** ~1.6 million
- **The Bronx:** ~1.4 million
- **Staten Island:** ~0.5 million

Total NYC population: Over 8.4 million
Rest of New York State: ~11 million

MANHATTAN: THE ICONIC ISLAND

Manhattan skyline. Image via depositphotos.com

A $24 ISLAND?

Manhattan was famously "purchased" from the Lenape people in 1626 for goods worth about 60 Dutch guilders, later estimated to equal about $24 at the time—roughly $1,000 in today's money. The trade likely included tools, cloth, and other goods.

Many historians believe the Lenape may have understood the agreement as shared land use, rather than a permanent sale of the island. A replica of the deed is displayed at the New-York Historical Society on Manhattan's Upper West Side.

BROADWAY BEGINNINGS

Broadway is New York City's oldest north-south route. It's also the longest street in Manhattan, stretching 33 miles (53 km) from Lower Manhattan all the way to Sleepy Hollow. It began as a Native American trail called Wickquasgeck Road and kept its winding path even as Manhattan adopted a rigid street grid in the 1800s.

Map showing Manhattan with Broadway cutting diagonally across the grid. Image via depositphotos.com

While most streets were laid out in straight lines and right angles, Broadway famously cuts diagonally across the grid, making it one of the only streets in Manhattan to defy the city's orderly design.

THE APOLLO'S LEGENDARY STAGE

The Apollo Theater in Harlem, Upper Manhattan, has launched the careers of legends including Ella Fitzgerald, James Brown, and Lauryn Hill. Its famous Amateur Night, which began in 1934, still gives performers a chance to win over a notoriously tough crowd. Getting booed off the Apollo stage has become a rite of passage in music history.

YIDDISH THEATER LIVES ON

New York City was once the global center of Yiddish theater, especially on Manhattan's Lower East Side, where dozens of theaters staged plays for Jewish immigrant audiences in the late 1800s and early 1900s. Today, that tradition continues through the National Yiddish Theater Folksbiene, founded in 1915. It is the longest continuously operating Yiddish theater company in the world and still stages productions in New York more than a century later.

ONE WORLD TRADE CENTER

Rising to a symbolic height of 1,776 feet (541 m)—a nod to the year the U.S. declared independence—One World Trade Center is the tallest building in the Western Hemisphere, and seventh tallest in the world. Built on the site of the original World Trade Center towers, it stands as a powerful symbol of resilience, freedom, and national pride. A 47-second elevator ride whisks visitors to the top while showing a time-lapse animation of New York City's skyline evolving from the 1500s to today.

> **Visitor Tip:** Book your ticket just before sunset to see the city transform from day to night, and don't miss the Sky Portal—a glass floor that gives you a vertigo-inducing peek 100 stories straight down.

BIGGER THAN A COUNTRY

Central Park spans 843 acres (341 hectares), making it larger than the entire country of Monaco. Designed in the 1850s by

Frederick Law Olmsted and Calvert Vaux, it was inspired by romantic European gardens and has become one of the most visited urban parks in the world.

Before the park was created, the land was home to communities including Seneca Village, a predominantly Black settlement whose residents were displaced during the park's construction.

There is even a hidden blockhouse fort from the War of 1812 tucked into the park's northern section.

MORE VISITORS THAN NATIONAL PARKS

Central Park receives around 42 million visitors annually—more than Yellowstone and the Grand Canyon combined. It's so spacious that it contains a zoo, a castle, and even a hidden manmade waterfall.

LINCOLN CENTER: A STAGE FOR THE WORLD

Lincoln Center for the Performing Arts is one of the most prestigious performing arts complexes in the world. Opened in 1962, it is home to the Metropolitan Opera, New York City Ballet, and the New York Philharmonic. The iconic plaza fountain has appeared in countless films and remains a gathering spot for everything from summer concerts to black-tie galas.

PACKED LIKE SARDINES

Manhattan has over 27,000 people per square mile. On weekdays, some neighborhoods reach densities of more than 170,000 people per square mile—imagine cramming the population of Iceland into just a few blocks!

TIMES SQUARE: THE BRIGHTEST BLOCK IN THE WORLD

Once called Longacre Square, Times Square got its current name in 1904 when *The New York Times* moved its headquarters to the area. Today, it's one of the most visited places on Earth—more than 330,000 people pass through daily. With towering LED billboards glowing 24/7 (by law!), it's so bright that the area is often called "the Crossroads of the World."

The famous New Year's Eve Ball Drop, when a glowing ball descends a pole atop One Times Square at midnight to mark the start of the new year, began in 1907 after fireworks were banned. The modern ball weighs nearly 12,000 pounds (about 5,440 kilograms) and sparkles with 2,688 crystals designed by Waterford Crystal and manufactured by Gillinder Glass.

Despite hosting one of the world's most famous celebrations, One Times Square itself is mostly empty inside today, with most of its value coming from the massive digital billboards that wrap around the building—some of the most expensive advertising spaces in the world.

> **Hidden Gem:** Just steps away is Gulliver's Gate, a whimsical world of miniatures that showcases tiny replicas from 40 countries on 5 continents on a scale of 1:87.

WHY NEW YORK'S ICONIC TAXIS ARE YELLOW

Not all New York City taxis are yellow—but the most iconic ones are. Yellow cabs are the city's officially licensed street-hail taxis, and the bright color was chosen because it's easy to spot in heavy traffic. Although yellow taxis didn't originate in New York, the city later standardized the color, helping turn the yellow cab into one of the most recognizable symbols of New York City.

THE TAXI MEDALLION SYSTEM

For decades, New York City strictly limited how many yellow taxis could operate by issuing metal taxi medallions. At their peak in the early 2010s, some medallions sold for more than $1 million each, making them more expensive than many homes. The system shaped the city's taxi industry for generations and helped cement yellow cabs as a regulated and tightly controlled part of New York life.

DID YOU KNOW?

Anonymized New York City taxi trip data has been used by researchers and urban planners to study traffic patterns, congestion, and commuting behavior. In a way, taxis have helped scientists better understand how the city actually moves.

FLATIRON WIND TROUBLE

The Flatiron Building. Photo by Nick Fewings
on Unsplash

The Flatiron Building's unique triangular shape creates dramatic wind tunnels. In the early 1900s, the gusts became infamous for flipping women's skirts, prompting police to chase away lingering gawkers. That's where the old slang term "23 skidoo" comes from—telling people to scram from 23rd Street!

DID YOU KNOW?

The Metropolitan Museum of Art in Manhattan houses over 2 million works of art—more than most national collections. Among them is the actual Temple of Dendur, an ancient Egyptian temple that was relocated block by block from the Nile to Fifth Avenue.

EMPIRE STATE BUILDING'S SPEEDY CONSTRUCTION

The Empire State Building was completed in just 410 days during the Great Depression, opening in 1931, an extraordinary pace for a skyscraper of its time.

WORLD'S TALLEST — AND UNIQUE ZIP CODE

When it opened, the Empire State Building was the tallest building in the world, and today it's so massive that it has its own ZIP code — 10118 — just for mail delivery.

1945 BOMBER CRASH AND REOPENING

On July 28, 1945, a U.S. Army B-25 Mitchell bomber called the *Old John Feather Merchant* crashed into the Empire State Building's north side between the 78th and 80th floors due to fog, killing 14 people and injuring many others. Despite the damage and fire, the building was reopened for business just two days later.

BETTY LOU OLIVER'S EXTRAORDINARY SURVIVAL

Elevator operator Betty Lou Oliver, then age 20, survived a 75-story elevator plunge after the 1945 Bomber crash damaged cables—and then went on to live for decades afterward. This remains the Guinness World Record for the longest elevator fall survived. She suffered severe injuries but made a remarkable recovery.

ICONIC LIGHTING TRADITION

Since adopting a color lighting system in 1976, the Empire State Building's lights change throughout the year to celebrate holidays, special events, cultural occasions, sports victories, and important causes, using millions of LED color combinations.

The lighting schedule is updated regularly and includes specific color schemes for days like Thanksgiving, Pride, worldwide observances, and even team colors for local sports occasions; residents and visitors can even text to receive real-time information about what each lighting represents.

> **Insider Secret:** Save your money and skip the 102nd floor. The 86th-floor observation deck is outdoors, offers even better views, and feels far more thrilling—especially after 9 p.m. when the lines are shorter and the skyline sparkles.

WALL STREET'S ORIGINS

Wall Street is named for a 12-foot wooden wall built in the 1600s by Dutch settlers to protect the colony of New Amsterdam. Though the wall came down in 1699, the name stuck—and the area became a global financial hub. Cobblestone remnants of the original Dutch roads remain nearby.

WALL STREET TODAY

Today, Wall Street is home to the New York Stock Exchange, the largest stock exchange in the world by market value. Just steps away stands the famous Charging Bull, installed in 1989 as a symbol of financial optimism and market strength. Originally placed overnight without permission, the 7,000-pound (3,175 kg) bronze bull quickly became one of the most photographed sculptures in New York City.

THE FINAL FOUR PHONE BOOTHS

Despite all the city's high-tech infrastructure, there are still four classic, full-length phone booths standing on the Upper West Side—preserved by popular demand. They've become a nostalgic photo stop for tourists and locals alike.

TOP OF THE ROCK

The observation deck at Rockefeller Center—familiarly known as Top of the Rock—offers one of the most stunning panoramic views in all of New York City. Unlike the Empire State Building's own observatory, this one includes the Empire State Building in its skyline shot, making it a favorite for photographers and skyline lovers alike. To the north, you'll see the treetops of Central Park stretch toward Harlem; to the south, Manhattan's iconic towers sparkle all the way to Lower Manhattan.

> **Best Experience:** Visit in December to catch a bird's-eye view of the dazzling Rockefeller Christmas Tree and skating rink below. For an unforgettable start to your day, book a special "Sunrise Experience" ticket for early access—watching the city awaken beneath you in the soft morning light is pure magic.

THE SECRET REACTOR

Columbia University operated a small nuclear reactor on its Manhattan campus from 1961 to 2021—quietly tucked away in a city that never knew it was there. It was mainly used for research and training, and it sat just a few blocks from busy Broadway.

STATUE OF LIBERTY: A SYMBOL OF FREEDOM IN THE HARBOR

Standing 305 feet 1 inch (93 meters) from the ground to the tip of the flame, the Statue of Liberty rises above New York Harbor as one of America's most famous landmarks. It stands on Liberty Island, federal property within the territorial jurisdiction of New York State, even though the island lies closer to New Jersey. The statue's seven crown rays are often said to represent the world's seven continents and seven seas, while the broken chains and shackles at her feet symbolize freedom from oppression.

> **Local Tips:** Official ferries depart from Battery Park in Manhattan *and* from Liberty State Park in New Jersey. If you're driving, the New Jersey departure point can be easier for parking. Your ticket also includes access to Ellis Island, home of the Immigration Museum. Crown access tickets sell out months in advance, so plan early!

THE BRONX: WHERE HIP-HOP WAS BORN

THE ONLY MAINLAND BOROUGH

The Bronx is the only NYC borough located on the mainland. It's named after Jonas Bronck, a Swedish settler whose farm sat along what is now the Bronx River. There's also a little-known waterfall—called Bronx River Falls—tucked into the Bronx Zoo grounds, right along the river.

BIRTHPLACE OF HIP-HOP

Hip-hop was born in the Bronx in 1973 at a back-to-school party at 1520 Sedgwick Avenue. DJ Kool Herc used two turntables to extend beats—creating the blueprint for modern hip-hop. The building is now a hip-hop landmark and sometimes hosts community events celebrating the genre's roots.

THE HOUSE THAT RUTH (AND A FEW MILLION FANS) BUILT

Yankee Stadium, located in the Bronx, opened in 1923 and quickly became one of the most iconic sports venues in the world—earning the nickname "The House That Ruth Built" after slugger Babe Ruth drew record crowds. It was the site of 26 Yankees World Series wins, a visit from Pope John Paul II, and countless legendary moments in baseball history.

Aerial view of Yankee Stadium in the Bronx. Photo via depositphotos.com

In 2009, the Yankees moved to a brand-new stadium just across the street. There, they have won one World Series Title. The new Yankee Stadium blends modern luxury with historic charm and even features a museum, a replica of Monument Park, and a "Great Hall" lined with towering banners of Yankee legends.

BALLPARK BITES

Yankee Stadium sells over 1 million hot dogs per season—more than any other Major League Baseball (MLB) park. Classic toppings include spicy brown mustard, sauerkraut, or sweet onion sauce. But fans can also find quirky eats like milkshakes topped with bacon or burgers served on glazed doughnuts.

WILD ABOUT ANIMALS

The Bronx Zoo spans 265 acres and houses over 6,000 animals. It's one of the largest metropolitan zoos in the world. The zoo is home to some unusual residents, including tree kangaroos, a snow leopard family, and even a colony of Madagascar hissing cockroaches.

SEASIDE SURPRISE

City Island in the Bronx feels like a New England fishing village. It's a go-to spot for seafood and beach-town charm. Legend has it the island was once considered as the location for the United Nations before Manhattan won out.

SCIENCE STARS OF THE BRONX

The Bronx is home to one of the most accomplished public high schools in the world: Bronx High School of Science. Founded in 1938, "Bronx Science" has produced nine Nobel Prize winners, more than any other secondary school on Earth.

Alumni include physicists Sheldon Glashow and Steven Weinberg (Class of 1950), who helped develop the Standard Model of particle physics, as well as Russell Hulse, whose research provided key evidence for gravitational waves. Not bad for a single high school.

DID YOU KNOW?

Pelham Bay Park is NYC's largest park at 2,772 acres—more than three times the size of Central Park. It includes historic landmarks like the Bartow-Pell Mansion and even has its own beach: Orchard Beach, nicknamed "the Bronx Riviera."

BROOKLYN: THE BRIDGE AND BEYOND

THE WOMAN WHO TOOK THE BRIDGE ACROSS THE FINISH LINE

When the Brooklyn Bridge opened in 1883, it was the longest suspension bridge in the world—and it wouldn't have been completed without Emily Warren Roebling.

After her husband—chief engineer Washington Roebling—became paralyzed, Emily stepped in to manage construction on his behalf. She studied engineering, relayed instructions, oversaw crews, and became the project's key field leader. When the bridge finally opened, she was the first to cross it—carrying a rooster in her lap as a symbol of triumph.

ELEPHANTS ON THE BRIDGE

To prove the Brooklyn Bridge was safe in 1884, P.T. Barnum led 21 elephants across it—including Jumbo. The stunt drew massive crowds and remains one of the most unusual traffic jams in the city's history.

FIRST ROLLER COASTER

Coney Island debuted the world's first roller coaster in 1884—the Switchback Railway. Riders paid 5 cents to travel at 6 mph. Early thrill-seekers lined up in long queues, and the ride's success helped turn Coney Island into America's playground.

PARK AND GARDEN GLORY

Like Central Park, both Prospect Park and the Brooklyn Botanic Garden were designed by Frederick Law Olmsted and Calvert Vaux. The Botanic Garden's cherry blossom festival is a spring highlight, and the park's Long Meadow is one of the longest uninterrupted stretches of meadow in any U.S. urban park.

SECRET SUBWAY TUNNEL

The Atlantic Avenue Tunnel beneath Brooklyn was built in 1844 for the Long Island Rail Road, making it one of the oldest railroad tunnels in the United States. The brick tunnel carried steam trains below street level along Atlantic Avenue before it was sealed around 1861.

Atlantic Avenue Tunnel. Photo by Vlad Rud, CC BY-SA 3.0, via Wikimedia Commons

In 1980, urban explorer Bob Diamond rediscovered the tunnel beneath a manhole cover while searching through old railroad records. The tunnel stretches about 1,400 feet (427 meters) and is often mistakenly called the world's oldest subway tunnel —even though it was originally built for trains, not subways.

Over the years, colorful legends have surrounded the tunnel, including rumors of secret Confederate schemes, hidden treasure, and even a supposed connection to Edgar Allan Poe—though these stories remain unproven.

FORMER CITY STATUS

Before joining Greater New York in 1898, Brooklyn was the fourth-largest city in the U.S. Yet today, some residents still say they're "going to the city" when heading to Manhattan. Brooklynites have long maintained a strong independent streak—and some even called the merger "the Great Mistake of 1898."

DID YOU KNOW?

The very first teddy bear was inspired by a cartoon of President Theodore "Teddy" Roosevelt refusing to shoot a captured bear on a hunting trip. The famous toy was later designed and sold by a Brooklyn candy shop owner named Morris Michtom, who displayed the original "Teddy's Bear" in his shop window in 1902—and the rest is snuggly history.

QUEENS: A WORLD IN ONE BOROUGH

MOST DIVERSE PLACE ON EARTH

Queens is considered the most ethnically and linguistically diverse urban area in the world, with over 160 languages spoken. Some neighborhoods even have restaurants serving food from more than 20 different countries within just a few blocks.

GLOBE OF THE FUTURE

The Unisphere in Flushing Meadows-Corona Park was built for the 1964 World's Fair. At 140 feet (43 m), it's the largest globe structure in the world.

The Unisphere. Photo via depositphotos.com

Nearby, several World's Fair relics remain scattered in the park, including the iconic Astro-View towers and the New York State Pavilion, once painted by Andy Warhol.

PANORAMA OF THE CITY OF NEW YORK

Just steps from the Unisphere inside the Queens Museum sits one of New York's most impressive hidden treasures: a massive scale model of all five boroughs.

Originally built for the 1964 World's Fair, the model spans nearly 10,000 square feet (930 sq m) and includes thousands of tiny buildings, bridges, and even miniature airports. It's periodically updated to reflect new construction, meaning you can literally see the entire city at your feet.

AIRPORTS WITH ATTITUDE

Queens is home to both JFK and LaGuardia airports, the only borough with major commercial airports and the only one with two. JFK handles over 60 million passengers a year.

LaGuardia, meanwhile, was once infamous for delays. But a recent $8 billion renovation added a striking new terminal featuring a waterfall wall, indoor garden, and expanded concourses, helping the airport operate far more efficiently.

TENNIS TITANS

The USTA Billie Jean King National Tennis Center hosts the U.S. Open. Arthur Ashe Stadium is the largest tennis venue in the world and has a retractable roof that closes in under seven minutes.

MUSICAL CRAFTSMANSHIP

Since 1870, the Steinway & Sons factory in Astoria has produced some of the world's finest pianos—each with over

12,000 parts. The factory includes a "piano vault" where climate and humidity are carefully controlled to preserve unfinished instruments.

A REAL LITTLE GUY FROM QUEENS

Before he was swinging between skyscrapers, Spider-Man's alter ego Peter Parker was a high school student from Forest Hills, Queens. The neighborhood still proudly claims the web-slinger as its most famous (fictional) resident.

URBAN AGRICULTURE

The Queens County Farm Museum is the city's largest remaining tract of farmland and still operates year-round. It even has a corn maze each fall and raises heritage breeds of livestock.

MOVIE MAGIC

Kaufman Astoria Studios. Photo by Jim.henderson, CC0, via Wikimedia Commons

Kaufman Astoria Studios is one of the oldest film studios in the U.S. and remains active today. It has hosted everything from early silent films to modern hits like "Orange Is the New Black."

IMMIGRATION STATION

Ellis Island wasn't the only entry point to the United States. In the early 20th century, thousands of immigrants were processed at the now-closed Ellis Island annex in Queens, near the docks of the East River.

Today, the borough continues to welcome newcomers from around the world—over 47% of Queens' residents were born outside the U.S.

DID YOU KNOW?

The New York Hall of Science was originally built for the 1964 World's Fair and still hosts hands-on exhibits today—including a mini-golf course made entirely of recycled materials.

STATEN ISLAND: THE HIDDEN GEM

FOREST IN THE CITY

The Staten Island Greenbelt covers nearly 3,000 acres and is home to deer, foxes, owls, and coyotes. Some trails even cross through neighborhoods, giving residents unexpected wildlife encounters right in their backyards.

FROM DUMP TO PARK

Freshkills Park is transforming a former landfill into one of the world's largest urban parks. Once known for towering piles of garbage, it's now home to migrating birds, tidal creeks, and ambitious plans for hiking trails and public art.

THE FREE FERRY

Staten Island Ferry. Photo via depositphotos.com

The Staten Island Ferry has been operating since 1905 and carries over 22 million passengers annually—for free! The 25-minute ride offers one of the best skyline and Statue of Liberty views in the entire city.

FARMING STILL LIVES HERE

Staten Island has some of NYC's last active farmland and farmers markets. In fact, Staten Island was once called "the borough of farms," and it's not unusual to spot scarecrows during fall harvest festivals—or even the occasional goat at a community event. One location—the Decker Farm—dates back to the 1600s, and is still operational today as part of a historic site.

SUNKEN SHIPS

The Staten Island Boat Graveyard holds dozens of rusting, decommissioned ships—fascinating for maritime history buffs and adventurous kayakers. It's one of the largest ship graveyards in the United States. Some of the vessels date back to World War I, and rumor has it that a few were featured in old Hollywood films as dramatic shipwreck sets.

TINY LIGHTHOUSE

The Staten Island Rear Range Lighthouse may be just 47 feet tall, but it's vital for navigation in the busy Kill Van Kull. At night, its beam lines up perfectly with its sister lighthouse to guide cargo ships through the narrow waterway. Despite its modest size, the lighthouse is so precisely aligned that ships use it like a landing strip—steering by sight through the channel as if threading a needle.

DID YOU KNOW?

Wild deer, turkeys, and coyotes roam Staten Island's woodlands and even backyards. Local residents sometimes spot flocks of wild turkeys strolling across suburban streets—a scene that feels more like rural New England than New York City.

SURPRISING FACTS ABOUT
THE CITY THAT NEVER SLEEPS

MIDNIGHT ART TAKEOVER

Every night from 11:57 p.m. to midnight, the massive digital billboards in Times Square synchronize to display contemporary art in what's called the "Midnight Moment." Since 2012, this three-minute digital exhibition has featured works by artists like Yoko Ono and Pipilotti Rist—turning Times Square into the world's largest (and most unexpected) digital art gallery.

THE DREAM HOUSE

Tucked away in a nondescript Tribeca building is the "Dream House," a sound and light installation created in 1993 by composer La Monte Young and artist Marian Zazeela. Visitors step into a space filled with magenta light and sustained sound frequencies—described by some as a meditative, out-of-body experience. It's open to the public but known mostly through word of mouth.

ELEVATOR TO THE MOON (ALMOST!)

New York City has approximately 70,000 elevators, making roughly 35 million trips every day—enough vertical travel to reach the moon and back twice in 24 hours. The average New Yorker waits about 16 to 20 seconds for each ride. Collectively, the city spends over 16 years per day just waiting for elevators.

A SLICE OF THE ACTION

New Yorkers eat an estimated 250,000 slices of pizza every day—over 91 million annually. For more than 50 years, the average price of a slice has closely tracked the cost of a subway fare, a strange economic phenomenon known as the "Pizza Principle."

OLDEST BUILDING IN MANHATTAN

Fraunces Tavern, built in 1719, is where George Washington gave his farewell speech to his officers. It narrowly avoided demolition and now operates as a museum and pub. The tavern has also played host to centuries of myths, including rumors of secret tunnels and spy meetings during the Revolutionary War. Some visitors even claim it's haunted by colonial-era spirits!

MANHATTANHENGE

Manhattanhenge. Photo via depositphotos.com

Twice a year, the setting sun aligns perfectly with Manhattan's east–west street grid, casting a golden glow down every cross street. Nicknamed "Manhattanhenge" by astrophysicist Neil deGrasse Tyson, it typically occurs around May 28–30 and July 11–13, though exact dates shift slightly each year. On these evenings, the sun appears to hover between skyscrapers in a dazzling display that draws massive crowds and amateur photographers, who block traffic for the perfect shot.

There's also a lesser-known sunrise version, which happens in early December and early January, when the rising sun aligns with the same street grid—though it's a much colder, sleepier spectacle that only the most die-hard early birds tend to catch.

A LOGO THAT LIFTED A CITY

The iconic "I ♥ NY" logo was sketched in 1977 on the back of an envelope during a taxi ride by designer Milton Glaser. He donated it to New York State for free as part of a campaign to boost tourism—and it went on to become one of the most recognizable logos in the world, a timeless symbol of the city's spirit.

MILTON GLASER: THE MAN BEHIND "I ♥ NY"

Milton Glaser shaped the visual identity of an entire era. He created the swirling, psychedelic Bob Dylan poster for the singer's Greatest Hits album, co-founded New York Magazine in 1968, and designed the Brooklyn Brewery logo that still graces bottles today.

After the tragedy of 9/11, Glaser updated his famous creation to say "I ♥ NY More Than Ever," adding a small black mark on the heart to honor the lives lost. In 2009, President Barack Obama awarded him the National Medal of Arts, the highest U.S. honor for creative achievement—cementing Glaser's place as a true New York legend.

THE WHISPERING GALLERY

Just outside the Oyster Bar inside Grand Central Terminal is the Whispering Gallery, a spot where sound behaves in a surprising way. Thanks to the gallery's curved, tiled arches, a soft whisper spoken into one corner can be heard clearly at the diagonally opposite corner, about 30 feet (9 m) away, while people standing in between hear almost nothing at all.

HIDDEN SPACES ABOVE GRAND CENTRAL

High above the Main Concourse is a secret tennis court, once used by wealthy New Yorkers and still in use today by invitation only. The terminal's iconic four-faced opal clock also hides a narrow staircase, believed to have led to private offices and passageways used by railway executives and VIPs in the station's early years.

THE CITY BELOW THE CITY

The New York City Subway includes 472 stations and about 665 miles (1,070 kilom) of track, making it one of the largest rapid-transit systems in the world. Hidden within the network are surprises like the long-closed City Hall station, famous for its elegant arches, skylights, and chandeliers that most riders never get to see.

UNDERGROUND SECRETS

In the early 1900s, NYC ran a 27-mile pneumatic mail tube system beneath the streets, zipping letters and small packages at nearly 30 miles per hour. It was so reliable that in 1913, the system moved over 90,000 letters a day. One cheeky employee even mailed a pickle to test the system's limits. The tubes were eventually shut down in 1953, but remnants still exist beneath the streets—and some sealed off stations remain visible to urban explorers.

A BRICK-LOAD OF BUILDINGS

New York City has over 1 million buildings, and the bricks used in the Empire State Building alone, more than 10 million, could stretch from Manhattan to San Francisco and back. Some buildings hide in plain sight: on West 58th Street in Manhattan, what appears to be a regular brownstone is actually a disguised subway ventilation shaft, complete with fake windows and doors to blend in with its neighbors.

DID YOU KNOW?

New York City's water travels more than 125 miles (201 km) from protected reservoirs in the Catskill Mountains to reach city taps. The system relies largely on gravity rather than pumps, delivering about 1 billion gallons of drinking water every day.

3

HIGHS, LOWS & OTHER NEW YORK GEOLOGY FACTS

New York's landscape wasn't just shaped by time. It was carved, crunched, frozen, and flipped by ancient forces. From billion-year-old bedrock to a mountain that's still rising today, the Empire State has one of the most fascinating geological stories in North America.

HOW BIG IS NEW YORK?

The state of New York spans about 54,556 square miles (141,300 km²), making it the 27th largest U.S. state. That's slightly larger than England (50,301 sq mi / 130,279 km²) and just a bit smaller than Nepal (56,956 sq mi / 147,516 km²). Pretty impressive for a state best known for one giant city!

It includes over 47,000 square miles (122,000 km²) of land and more than 7,400 square miles (19,200 km²) of water.

From east to west, the state stretches about 330 miles (531 km), roughly the same as the distance from Washington, D.C., to Boston, Massachusetts.

From north to south, it runs about 300 miles (483 km), similar to the drive from Philadelphia, Pennsylvania, to Richmond, Virginia.

THE HIGHEST POINT: MOUNT MARCY

The tallest point in New York is Mount Marcy, located in the Adirondack High Peaks region. It rises 5,344 feet (1,629 m) above sea level. The Mohawk people called it "Tahawus," meaning cloud-splitter. Climbing Mount Marcy is no walk in the park—it's a 14–15-mile (22–24 km) round-trip hike that takes most people 7–10 hours. But the views from the top? Totally worth it.

THE ADIRONDACK HIGH PEAKS

Mount Marcy is the tallest of 46 mountains in the Adirondacks that early surveyors believed were all over 4,000 feet (1,219 m). Later measurements showed a few fall just short of that height, but the original list stuck. Today, hikers who summit all 46 are proudly known as "Adirondack 46ers."

THE LOWEST POINT

New York's lowest natural point is sea level, where it meets the Atlantic Ocean. But here's a surprising twist: some skyscrapers in Manhattan have foundations that extend 80 feet (24 m) below sea level.

NEW YORK'S DEEPEST LAKE

Seneca Lake, one of the Finger Lakes, plunges to a depth of 618 feet (188 m), making it the deepest lake entirely within New York State. While Lakes Ontario and Erie are deeper overall, they're shared with Canada. Seneca Lake's bottom even lies below sea level!

GLACIAL HISTORY

Much of New York's unique landscape was shaped by massive glaciers during the last Ice Age. Around 10,000 years ago, mile-thick ice sheets scraped across the land, carving valleys, lakes, and ridges as they went. Long Island is one big leftover from this glacial action. It's a terminal moraine, made of sand, gravel, and rocks pushed there by glaciers. That's why it's shaped like a long fish tail, stretching 118 miles (190 km) into the Atlantic Ocean.

NATURAL LAND REGIONS OF NEW YORK

Geologists divide New York into several major landform regions, each with its own unique landscape and geological history:

- **Atlantic Coastal Plain** – Includes Long Island and sandy low-lying areas.
- **Appalachian Highlands** – Home to the Catskill mountains that have been shaped by erosion over millions of years.
- **Adirondack Mountains** – A massive dome of ancient rock that's still slowly rising today.
- **Erie-Ontario Lowlands** – Flat lands around Lakes Erie and Ontario, formed by glacial activity.
- **St. Lawrence–Champlain Lowlands** – Bordering Canada, these lowlands include river valleys and rolling plains.

ANCIENT ROOTS

The Adirondack Mountains are home to some of the oldest exposed rocks in the entire world—more than one billion years old. These rocks formed deep underground and were slowly pushed to the surface by powerful tectonic forces. To put it in perspective: these rocks were already ancient before dinosaurs ever walked the Earth!

SALT BENEATH THE STATE

Western New York sits on top of some of the thickest underground salt beds in the U.S., laid down over 400 million years ago when the area was covered by a shallow sea.

In some spots, these salt layers reach 2,000 feet (610 m) thick. This hidden resource is incredibly valuable—salt has been mined here for centuries to preserve food, de-ice roads in winter, and even help make certain chemicals. Today, giant underground salt mines still operate across the region.

MANHATTAN SCHIST: THE ROCK THAT HOLDS UP A CITY

New York City's skyline is only possible because of what lies below it. Deep underground is Manhattan Schist—a tough, glittery rock formed about 450 million years ago.

It's so strong that builders anchor skyscrapers directly into it, giving the city's tallest towers the solid foundation they need to soar.

HERKIMER "DIAMONDS"

They may not be real diamonds, but these sparkling quartz crystals from Herkimer County sure look the part! Formed around 500 million years ago, Herkimer "diamonds" are known for their incredible clarity and natural faceted points—almost like nature polished them just for show. They're a favorite among collectors and rockhounds alike.

ANCIENT IMPACTS & GEOLOGICAL SURPRISES

New York's landscape hides some jaw-dropping geological secrets. Panther Mountain in the Catskills was built atop a 6-

mile-wide (about 9.7 kilom) meteor crater, formed roughly 386 million years ago—now completely buried beneath ancient rock layers.

At Taughannock Falls near the Finger Lakes, the plunge pool is so deep it dips below sea level, even though it's hundreds of miles inland and high above sea level at the surface.

The Palisades, those striking cliffs along the Hudson River, were created around 200 million years ago when molten magma forced its way through sandstone and hardened into tough diabase rock. And if you want to walk through truly ancient time, head to Ausable Chasm in northeastern New York—where billion-year-old rock walls rise around you.

SHAKY GROUND

Yes, New York does get earthquakes. Most of the state's seismic activity comes from the Ramapo Fault System, which cuts through the Hudson Highlands. While large earthquakes are rare, small tremors are fairly common.

RISING MOUNTAINS

The Adirondack Mountains are on the move; slowly rising at a rate of about 0.08 inches (2 mm) per year. That makes them among the fastest-growing mountains in the world.

And thanks to a process called post-glacial rebound, the land is still springing back from the weight of ancient glaciers, rising about 4 to 5 inches (10 to 13 cm) every 100 years.

DID YOU KNOW?

Seneca Lake is so deep and calm that the U.S. Navy has used it since the 1950s to test sonar equipment. The water is clear and still enough to serve as a natural lab for underwater acoustics—earning it the nickname "the Navy's freshwater lab."

4

NEW YORK'S NATURAL WONDERS

Skyscrapers might steal the spotlight, but New York's true showstoppers are its wild rivers, deep gorges, ancient forests, and glacial lakes. From the crashing waterfalls of Ithaca to the island-filled St. Lawrence River, the Empire State is bursting with natural beauty.

LAKES, WATERFALLS & WILD RIVERS

WATER, WATER EVERYWHERE

New York is home to more than 7,600 freshwater lakes, ponds, and reservoirs, along with over 70,000 miles (112,600 km) of rivers and streams.

The state also has 130 miles (209 km) of Atlantic Ocean coastline and shares shores with two of the Great Lakes: Lake Erie and Lake Ontario.

THE FINGER LAKES: NATURE'S HANDPRINT

In central New York, a group of eleven long, narrow lakes stretch across the land like the fingers of a hand. These lakes were carved by glaciers during the last Ice Age roughly 15,000–20,000 years ago, as massive ice sheets slowly retreated from the region.

Map of New York showing Finger Lakes. Image via
depositphotos.com

The two largest, Seneca and Cayuga, are both long and deep.
Cayuga runs 38 miles (61 km) in length, while Seneca Lake
plunges 618 feet (188 m) at its deepest point, with its bottom
sitting below sea level.

TAUGHANNOCK FALLS: TALLER THAN NIAGARA

Located near Ithaca, Taughannock Falls plummets 215 feet (66
m), that's nearly 40 feet (12 m) taller than Niagara Falls! It's the
tallest free-falling waterfall east of the Rocky Mountains, and
you can walk right up to its misty base.

KAATERSKILL FALLS: A ROMANTIC ERA ICON

Nestled in the Catskills, Kaaterskill Falls drops a total of 260 feet (79 m) in two dramatic tiers. This picturesque cascade has been featured in paintings, poems, and travel journals since the 1800s.

A WATERFALL WONDERLAND

New York State boasts more than 2,000 waterfalls. From roaring giants to secret streams tucked into quiet forest corners, the state offers something for every waterfall chaser.

THE GORGE-OUS SIDE OF ITHACA

Within 10 miles (16 km) of downtown Ithaca, you'll find over 150 waterfalls and gorges, shaped by glaciers and flowing water. Carved through layers of shale and sandstone, these dramatic ravines create stunning hiking trails, scenic overlooks, and even popular swimming spots.

Ithaca's waterfall-filled landscape began forming more than 10,000 years ago, when glacial meltwater surged through the region.

THE HUDSON RIVER: TIDAL AND TIMELESS

The lower Hudson River is technically a drowned glacial valley, often described as a fjord. During the last Ice Age, glaciers carved a deep channel through the Hudson Valley. When the ice melted and sea levels rose, Atlantic water flooded the valley, creating the tidal river we see today.

Ocean-going ships can sail all the way to Albany, over 150 miles (241 km) inland. The river has been a major shipping route for centuries and helped make New York City one of the world's busiest ports.

SARATOGA SPRINGS: NATURE'S MINERAL SPA

Saratoga Springs is bubbling with history—literally. Its naturally fizzy mineral waters rise through cracks in ancient rock, picking up minerals like calcium and sodium. Indigenous peoples believed in its healing powers, and by the 1800s, "taking the waters" became all the rage. Visitors came for sips, soaks, and even carbonated baths—and you still can partake of these customs today.

SALT CITY AND ANCIENT SEAS

In the 1800s, Syracuse was the leading salt producer in the United States. The salt came from brine springs around Onondaga Lake, remnants of an ancient sea that once covered the region. Syracuse still carries the nickname "Salt City."

FORESTS, PARKS & PROTECTED LANDS

A WILDERNESS STATE

Despite its towering skyline, New York is also a land of wild places. Nearly 20% of the state is protected as public forests, parks, and wildlife areas—an area larger than the entire country of Denmark. These lands include everything from quiet pine forests and rugged mountains to sandy coastal dunes and alpine meadows.

ADIRONDACK PARK: OVERSHADOWING NATIONAL PARKS

Adirondack Park covers 6 million acres (2.4 million hectares). Its mix of public and private land, including towns, lakes, and forests, is larger than Yellowstone, Yosemite, Grand Canyon, Glacier, and Olympic National Parks combined! About 2.6

million acres are "Forever Wild"—a unique constitutional protection.

FOREVER WILD

Article XIV of the New York State Constitution, adopted in 1894, states that lands in the Adirondack and Catskill Forest Preserves "shall be forever kept as wild forest lands." This protection is stronger than many U.S. national parks and can only be changed by a constitutional amendment.

OLD-GROWTH SURVIVORS

While much of the East Coast was cleared for farming, New York has rare pockets of old-growth forest. The Five Ponds Wilderness has trees over 400 years old. In Zoar Valley near Buffalo, hardwoods reach heights of 150 feet (46 m), making it one of the tallest hardwood forests in the Northeast.

DID YOU KNOW?

New York's old-growth forests cover less than 0.5% of the state's land area. Many survived simply because they were too remote, too rocky, or seen as sacred places that people chose not to disturb.

CATSKILL PARK: THE FIRST WILDERNESS GETAWAY

Catskill Park became one of the country's first accessible wilderness escapes when it was established in 1904, helping spark the American conservation movement. Just 100 miles (160 km) from New York City, it spans 700,000 acres (283,000 hectares), and inspired the Hudson River School of landscape painters.

GATEWAY TO NATURE

Gateway National Recreation Area protects over 27,000 acres (10,900 hectares) of beaches, wetlands, and wildlife habitats around New York Harbor—including Jamaica Bay Wildlife Refuge in Queens and Sandy Hook across the bay in New Jersey. It's a bird-watcher's paradise and one of the few National Park sites you can reach by subway.

NIAGARA FALLS: AMERICA'S FIRST STATE PARK

Many visitors are surprised to learn that Niagara Falls isn't a national park. Rather, it's a state park. In fact, it's the very first state park in the United States.

In the 1800s, private businesses had fenced off much of the land around the falls. Visitors had to pay just to catch a glimpse. That changed in 1885, when landscape architect Frederick Law Olmsted led a movement to preserve the area and return it to the public. Thanks to his efforts, Niagara Falls State Park was born—31 years before the National Park Service even existed!

A STATE PARK POWERHOUSE

New York isn't just home to America's first state park—it has one of the largest and busiest state park systems in the country. With more than 250 state parks and historic sites, New York offers everything from beaches and waterfalls to castles, caves, and mountain trails.

Together, these parks welcome over 79 million visitors each year, rivaling or exceeding attendance at iconic destinations like Great Smoky Mountains National Park, Acadia National Park, and Shenandoah National Park.

FOREST COMEBACK

By the mid-1800s, over 75% of New York's forests had been cut down. Today, more than 60% of the state is forested once again. This natural recovery provides clean water, wildlife habitat, and helps fight climate change by storing carbon.

THE EMPIRE STATE TRAIL

Completed in 2020, the Empire State Trail is one of the longest multi-use trails in the U.S., stretching 750 miles (1,207 km). It links New York City north to the Canadian border and east to west from Albany to Buffalo. The trail weaves together greenways, canal paths, and scenic byways—perfect for walking, running, and cycling adventures across the state.

DID YOU KNOW?

The Adirondack Park alone contains over 30,000 miles (48,280 km) of rivers and streams—enough to circle the Earth more than once!

MOUNTAINS, RIDGES & CANYONS

GORGES, CHASMS AND WILD CANYONS

The Ausable Chasm is a 150-foot-deep sandstone gorge in the northeastern Adirondacks, nicknamed the "Grand Canyon of the East." Letchworth State Park also lays claim to that title, with a gorge up to 600 feet (183 m) deep carved by the Genesee River.

THE SHAWANGUNKS: CLIFFS AND SKY LAKES

View of Hudson Valley from Shawangunk Mountains. Photo via depositphotos.com

The Shawangunk Mountains (often called the "Gunks") rise above the Hudson Valley with dramatic white cliffs and rare sky lakes—small lakes perched high on the mountaintops. Known worldwide among rock climbers, the area also features dwarf pine barrens and scenic hiking trails through protected natural areas such as Minnewaska State Park Preserve and the Mohonk Preserve.

MONTAUK POINT

At the far eastern tip of Long Island, Montauk Point's dramatic bluffs meet the Atlantic Ocean. Its iconic light-house, commissioned by George Washington, marks the end of the 118-mile (190 km) glacial landform that is Long Island.

THE APPALACHIAN TRAIL

The Appalachian Trail runs about 90 miles (145 km) through New York. It includes the lowest point on the entire trail—just 124 feet (38 m) above sea level—at Bear Mountain Bridge. This area also includes the first section of the trail ever built, completed in 1923. Hikers here pass through forests, across ridges, and even near a train stop where they can ride directly into Manhattan.

DID YOU KNOW?

During construction of the Appalachian Trail steps at Bear Mountain, workers used hand tools and stone quarried on-site. Some of the steps weigh over 1,000 pounds (450 kg)—that's about as much as a grand piano or a full-grown polar bear!

ISLANDS, COASTS & HIDDEN ECOSYSTEMS

THE THOUSAND ISLANDS

The Thousand Islands region contains 1,864 islands where the St. Lawrence River meets Lake Ontario. To count as an island, a landmass must remain above water year-round and support at least one living tree. Some islands there are no bigger than a bed, while others hold castles.

LAKE GEORGE: THE QUEEN OF AMERICAN LAKES

Lake George stretches 32 miles (51.5 km) through the southeastern Adirondacks. With over 170 islands and exceptionally clear waters, it has long been celebrated for its beauty. Thomas Jefferson once called it "the most beautiful water I ever saw."

LONG ISLAND'S WILD SIDE

View from the Fire Island Lighthouse. Photo via depositphotos.com

Eastern Long Island is home to surprising wilderness. Fire Island National Seashore protects 32 miles (51.5 km) of barrier island with dunes, beaches, and forests. The Otis Pike High Dune Wilderness is New York's only federally designated wilderness area.

THE SUNKEN FOREST

Fire Island's Sunken Forest is one of the rarest holly forests in the world. Sheltered behind dunes, this ancient woodland features American holly trees over 300 years old. It's called "sunken" because the forest floor sits lower than the surrounding dunes.

DID YOU KNOW?

New York has more state-designated wilderness land than any other state east of the Mississippi River—including over 1 million acres (405,000 hectares) in the Adirondacks and Catskills alone.

5

CRAZY & RECORD-BREAKING WEATHER OF NEW YORK STATE

New York's weather doesn't do boring. From blizzards that shut down cities to heatwaves that melt asphalt, this state has seen it all—and then some. Whether you're watching leaves fall or icicles form, the Empire State's climate comes with big swings, big stories, and even bigger snowdrifts. Here's a wild ride through the state's most extreme forecasts.

FOUR SEASONS, BIG PERSONALITY

NEW YORK'S FOUR SEASONS
New York experiences all four distinct seasons, each bringing its own unique character to the state.

Spring fills Brooklyn's parks with blooming cherry blossoms and wakes up apple orchards in the Hudson Valley.

Summers can be hot and sticky, especially in New York City, where the pavement seems to radiate heat.

Autumn transforms the landscape into a painter's palette, with vibrant foliage in the Adirondacks and Catskills.

Winters range from light dustings in New York City to

towering lake-effect snowstorms in western and northern parts of the state.

NEW YORK'S AVERAGE TEMPERATURES

The state's wide variety of landscapes means temperatures can vary dramatically. In upstate New York, winter temperatures often hover between 5°F and 25°F (-15°C to -4°C), while New York City stays milder at 25°F to 40°F (-4°C to 4°C).

Summer temperatures across the state generally fall between 70°F and 85°F (21°C to 29°C), but NYC frequently sees days that soar above 90°F (32°C), with humidity that can hug you like a wet blanket.

NEW YORK'S HOTTEST DAY

The hottest temperature ever recorded in New York State was a sweltering 108°F (42.2°C) in Troy on July 22, 1926. This nearly century-old record has endured through countless modern heatwaves. Residents described the air as so thick and heavy that it felt impossible to breathe, and city streets reportedly softened in the extreme heat.

NEW YORK'S COLDEST DAY

On February 9, 1934, the Adirondacks saw temperatures plunge to a bone-chilling -52°F (-46.7°C) at Stillwater Reservoir. Lakes and rivers froze so completely that in some places the ice didn't fully melt until early summer. Locals bundled up in multiple layers, but vehicles and machinery struggled to function in the extreme cold.

EXTREME TEMPERATURE SWINGS

New York's record temperatures span an astonishing 160°F (nearly 89°C)—from -52°F (-47°C) to 108°F (42°C). That's a range that rivals entire countries! This wild swing reflects the state's diverse climate zones, from the snowy shores of the Great Lakes to the milder Atlantic coast.

HEAT ISLANDS IN THE CONCRETE JUNGLE

New York City is often much warmer than its surrounding suburbs, thanks to the "urban heat island" effect. During summer heatwaves, Manhattan nights can stay up to 22°F (12°C) hotter than nearby rural areas because the concrete and asphalt trap heat. This makes NYC's summer nights feel more like tropical evenings than typical Northeastern weather.

DID YOU KNOW?

In December 1980, the small Adirondack town of Old Forge experienced an astonishing 24-hour temperature drop of 81°F (45°C)—plummeting from a mild 44°F (7°C) to a brutal -37°F (-38°C) overnight.

SNOWFALL LEGENDS

THE BLIZZARD OF 1888

The Great Blizzard of 1888 buried New York City in drifts so high they reached second-story windows. Trains and streetcars stopped running, and stranded New Yorkers had to tunnel through snow to leave their homes. In the Catskills, snow piled up an unbelievable 50 feet (15 m) in some places, cutting off entire towns for days!

The Great Blizzard of 1888. Photo taken in Brooklyn. Photo via Brooklyn Museum, No restrictions, via Wikimedia Commons

BUFFALO'S LEGENDARY SNOWFALL

Thanks to lake-effect snow—when cold air sweeps across the warmer waters of the Great Lakes and dumps heavy snow on nearby towns— Buffalo, New York gets hammered with an average of 95 inches (241 cm) of snow each year.

In November 2014, parts of Erie County, New York south of the city were buried under more than 7 feet (2.1 m) of snow in just 48 hours. Roofs collapsed, roads vanished, and residents had to climb out of second-story windows.

SURPRISING SNOWFALL RECORD

Oddly enough, Buffalo's biggest one-day snowfall didn't come from lake-effect storms at all. On December 10, 1995, a rare nor'easter dumped nearly 38 inches of snow (97 cm) in just 24 hours.

A nor'easter is a powerful storm that forms along the U.S. East Coast, named for the strong northeast winds it brings inland. These storms pull moist air from the Atlantic Ocean and can cause heavy snow, rain, strong winds, and coastal flooding—especially when cold air is already in place.

The city was completely paralyzed, and emergency crews struggled to reach neighborhoods buried under the sudden onslaught.

THE CHAMPION OF SNOW: TUG HILL PLATEAU

The Tug Hill Plateau near Lake Ontario holds the crown for New York's snowiest spot. In 2007, the town of Redfield in Oswego County saw a staggering 141.3 inches (359 cm) of snow in just 10 days. That's over 11 feet (3.4 m)—enough to completely bury a one-story house!

THE "SNOW BELT" EFFECT

Communities separated by just 20 miles (32 km) can have a 100-inch (254 cm) difference in annual snowfall due to lake-effect snow bands. One town might be buried under several feet (over a meter) of snow, while the next enjoys sunshine and clear skies on the very same day.

ICE STORMS & FREEZES

THE GREAT ICE STORM OF 1998

In January 1998, a historic ice storm coated parts of northern New York in up to 4 inches (10 cm) of solid ice. Power lines snapped under the weight, leaving hundreds of thousands without electricity for weeks in frigid conditions. Roads turned into glassy sheets, making travel nearly impossible.

ICE BY THE TON

During that same storm, some power lines were weighed down by more than three tons (2,700 kg) of ice—enough weight to topple steel towers. Entire forests were devastated as trees cracked and fell under the extreme pressure of the frozen buildup.

BURIED TO STAY POWERED

In dense parts of New York City, especially Manhattan, many power lines run underground rather than overhead. This protects them from ice, wind, and falling branches during winter storms.

In contrast, much of upstate New York still relies on above-ground lines, which are more vulnerable during major ice events like the devastating storm of 1998.

NORTH COUNTRY DEEP FREEZE

Saranac Lake, known as "The Icebox of the Nation," frequently plunges below -30°F (-34°C) in the winter. Locals are so used to the brutal cold that they host a Winter Carnival every February, complete with an ice palace built entirely from frozen blocks cut from the lake.

CENTRAL PARK WEATHER DETECTIVES

Central Park has been recording official weather data since 1869, making it one of the longest-running urban climate records in the world. These measurements help scientists track long-term trends like rising temperatures and shifting snowfall patterns due to climate change.

WILD WEATHER ODDITIES

THUNDERSNOW CAPITAL

Buffalo and Watertown are among the few places in the U.S. where "thundersnow" is a regular occurrence. During intense lake-effect storms, you can hear booming thunder while snow falls at rates of up to 4 inches (10 cm) per hour—turning the sky an eerie, glowing white.

TORNADO ALLEY? NOT QUITE

New York isn't famous for tornadoes, but the state still sees about 10 per year. In 1970, an F3 tornado (winds up to 206 mph or 332 km/h) tore through Franklin Grove, and in 2018, an EF2 (winds up to 135 mph or 217 km/h) struck near Newburgh —surprising residents who didn't expect such intense weather.

MANHATTAN TWISTER

In August 2007, a rare tornado touched down in Brooklyn and Queens—the first Brooklyn tornado since 1889! It tore roofs off homes and uprooted hundreds of trees in just a few minutes, reminding New Yorkers that even the city isn't immune to unexpected twisters.

MICROCLIMATES OF THE FINGER LAKES

The deep, glacial Finger Lakes act like natural heat reservoirs, storing warmth during the summer and slowly releasing it in colder months. This moderates nearby temperatures and can create differences of up to 10°F (6°C) from one side of a lake to the other. The slightly warmer conditions help protect grapevines from frost, which is why the region is famous for its vineyards and wineries despite harsh upstate winters.

THE STRANGE CASE OF THE MOHAWK VALLEY

The Mohawk Valley between Albany and Utica has a strange weather quirk—storms often split around it, leaving a narrow dry corridor while surrounding towns get soaked. Meteorologists still debate exactly why this happens, but locals see it as their lucky weather shield.

FALL COLORS & BILLION-DOLLAR LEAVES

THE AUTUMN SPECTACLE AND "LEAF PEEPERS"

Autumn leaves in the Catskills mountains. Photo via depositphotos.com

Every fall, a wave of brilliant color sweeps southward from the Adirondacks to New York City over about six weeks. Leaf peepers flock to the Catskills and Hudson Valley to catch the peak colors, turning quiet mountain towns into bustling seasonal hotspots.

BILLION-DOLLAR LEAVES

Autumn foliage isn't just beautiful—it's big business. Fall tourism generates over $1 billion annually for New York's economy, with some towns seeing their populations surge by 500% during peak weekends. Hotels and inns book up months in advance for this seasonal spectacle.

WEATHER'S ROLE IN FOLIAGE

The best red and orange colors come from sunny days and crisp, cool nights, which boost anthocyanin pigment production in leaves. A rainy or warm autumn can dull the show, while perfect weather turns the forests into a dazzling mosaic.

THE OLYMPIC TRAIL SCENIC BYWAY

Driving the Olympic Trail Scenic Byway through the Adirondack Park during peak foliage is like traveling through a living rainbow. This 6-million-acre park offers layer upon layer of autumn color, from deep burgundy oaks to blazing orange sugar maples.

DID YOU KNOW?

Different trees in New York contribute different colors—sugar maples turn brilliant red and orange, birches shine bright yellow, and oaks deepen to rich burgundy. Together, they create one of the most vibrant and diverse fall foliage displays in the entire world.

CLIMATE QUIRKS & LOCAL LORE

THE MAPLE SYRUP EFFECT

Maple syrup season in New York usually runs from late February through March, when freezing nights followed by warmer daytime temperatures cause sap to flow from sugar maple trees. In recent years, climate change has shifted the season earlier—sometimes starting in February or even late January in some areas—altering a tradition that has lasted for generations.

SUBWAY TEMPERATURE SWINGS

New York City's subway stations have their own mini climate. In summer, some underground stations hit a sweltering 106°F (41°C), while in winter they stay surprisingly warm, creating an unintentional year-round heating system for commuters.

STORM NAMES, NEW YORK STYLE

Before winter storms were unofficially named by The Weather Channel, New Yorkers and local media came up with their own dramatic nicknames. Blizzards were called things like "Snowpocalypse" and "Snoverkill," showing off the city's mix of humor, grit, and flair for turning chaos into headlines.

STORM CHASING, NEW YORK STYLE

In western New York, meteorology students and scientists track lake-effect snow bands much like tornado chasers track twisters. Using radar and mobile weather labs, they study how these narrow and intense snowstorms develop and move. It is not uncommon for several feet of snow to fall in one town while skies stay blue just a few miles away.

WEATHER DISASTERS & RESILIENCE

HURRICANE SANDY

When Hurricane Sandy struck New York in 2012, a storm surge of about 14 feet (4.3 m) flooded Lower Manhattan and large sections of the city's waterfront. Coastal neighborhoods across New York City and Long Island were heavily damaged, while high winds and flooding caused power outages and damage in parts of the Hudson Valley and elsewhere in the state.

The storm caused about $19 billion in damage in New York City alone, shut down the subway system, and left some neighborhoods without power for weeks.

HURRICANE IRENE

The year before, Hurricane Irene devastated mountain towns in the Catskills and Adirondacks. Some areas saw over 15 inches (38 cm) of rain, turning peaceful streams into raging torrents that washed away roads, bridges, and even entire homes!

RAGING WATERS

During Irene, Schoharie Creek rose an incredible 17 feet (5.2 m) in just 12 hours. The sudden flooding swept away 150-year-old covered bridges and forever changed the landscape of small valley communities.

WEATHER-PROOF INFRASTRUCTURE

After Hurricane Sandy struck in 2012, New York City took major steps to protect itself from future storms. Marine flood doors were added to subway entrances in flood-prone areas, and many buildings moved power systems out of basements to higher floors where they would be safer from rising water.

Massive steel floodgates were also installed at vehicle tunnels, including the Queens–Midtown Tunnel. These doors can be sealed shut before major storms, helping prevent storm surge from flooding the tunnels and crippling transportation across the city.

Many of the upgrades made after Sandy have already proven useful. During more recent storms, flood doors kept some subway stations dry, and buildings that moved their power systems higher avoided outages that once shut them down. Still, heavy rainfall and flash floods remain a major challenge.

DID YOU KNOW?

Before refrigeration, the Hudson River ice harvesting industry was a winter powerhouse. In the 1800s, it produced over 3 million tons of ice annually, supplying New York City and beyond with natural ice for homes, restaurants, and even breweries.

6

NEW YORK'S WILDLIFE & ANIMAL FACTS

From black bears in the mountains to sharks off the coast, New York is teeming with animals both wild and wonderfully weird. Some are state symbols, others are elusive legends, and a few have even gone viral. Whether they fly, swim, slither, or scurry, here's a closer look at the creatures who also call the Empire State home.

OFFICIAL ANIMALS OF NEW YORK

NEW YORK'S STATE ANIMAL: THE BEAVER

The North American beaver became New York's official state mammal in 1975. Once nearly wiped out by the fur trade, beavers were reintroduced in the early 1900s and now number more than 60,000 across the state. Their image appears on the official seal of New York City, an ode to their historic economic importance.

THE BEAVER'S ENGINEERING SKILLS

Beavers transform entire landscapes through their dam-building. These wetland engineers create ponds that support fish, amphibians, birds, and plants, and also help reduce erosion and improve water quality. Some beaver dams in New York have stretched over 500 feet long!

NEW YORK'S STATE FISH: THE BROOK TROUT

The brook trout was named New York's state fish in 1975. This cold-loving native species thrives only in the cleanest, coldest waters and has become a key indicator of stream health. Sadly, brook trout have disappeared from about 90% of their historic Adirondack range due to pollution, warming temperatures, and invasive species.

NEW YORK'S STATE BIRD: THE EASTERN BLUEBIRD

Designated the state bird in 1970, the Eastern bluebird saw sharp population declines in the 20th century due to habitat loss and competition from invasive starlings. Conservationists launched massive nest box campaigns that helped bring these colorful songbirds back across the state.

NEW YORK'S STATE REPTILE: THE SNAPPING TURTLE

The common snapping turtle became New York's official state reptile in 2006. These prehistoric-looking turtles can live over 70 years and weigh up to 35 pounds (16 kg), about the size of a medium-sized dog. Despite their powerful jaws, they are shy and avoid confrontation unless provoked.

NEW YORK'S STATE INSECT: THE NINE-SPOTTED LADYBUG

In 1989, New York named the nine-spotted ladybug its state insect. Ironically, it was just as the species was disappearing. Once the most common ladybug in the state, it vanished from the landscape for decades before being rediscovered on an organic farm on Long Island in 2011.

NEW YORK'S STATE BUTTERFLY: THE RED-SPOTTED PURPLE

Named the official state butterfly in 2006, the red-spotted

purple has shimmering blue wings and brick-red spots, making it one of the most eye-catching butterflies fluttering through New York's woodlands. This butterfly is a master mimic. It looks like toxic species, helping it avoid predators.

NEW YORK'S STATE SHELL: THE BAY SCALLOP

The bay scallop became the state shell in 1988. Once a staple of Long Island's coastal fisheries, the species suffered devastating population losses due to brown tide algal blooms (rapid overgrowths of microscopic algae) in the 1980s. Restoration efforts are helping the scallop make a cautious comeback.

NEW YORK'S STATE FRESHWATER FISH: THE BROOK TROUT

In addition to its overall status, the brook trout is specifically recognized as the state's freshwater fish. This designation highlights the species' importance to New York's natural heritage and the need to protect its fragile cold-water habitats.

NEW YORK'S STATE SALTWATER FISH: THE STRIPED BASS

The striped bass became New York's official saltwater fish in 2006. These powerful migratory fish can live for decades and grow over 50 pounds (about 23 kilograms). Each spring they return from the Atlantic to spawn in the freshwater reaches of the Hudson River, an ecological event and fishing season eagerly awaited each year.

NOTABLE MAMMALS & PREDATORS

THE BLACK BEAR COMEBACK

Black bears have made an impressive recovery in New York,

with populations now estimated at 6,000 to 8,000. Once confined to the remote Adirondacks and Catskills, they now roam much of the state. Adult males can weigh over 500 pounds (227 kg), about as much as a vending machine, and some even exceed 700 pounds (318 kg).

EASTERN COYOTES: THE COYWOLF DEBATE

New York's eastern coyotes are hybrids, with DNA from multiple canids, including western coyotes, eastern wolves, and domestic dogs. Adults typically weigh 35 to 55 pounds (16 to 25 kg), similar to a Labrador retriever, but they look lankier and more fox-like. Known for their eerie howls, these coyotes are now found in every state county, and even in Central Park!

DID YOU KNOW?

A coyote once made its way onto the roof of a bar in Queens and had to be tranquilized by the NYPD Emergency Services Unit. Locals nicknamed it "Wile E.," and it was safely relocated upstate.

THE FISHER: PORCUPINE HUNTER EXTRAOR-DINAIRE

Despite its name, the fisher rarely eats fish. This cat-sized member of the weasel family is a predator that can grow up to 40 inches (1 meter) long, including its tail. That's roughly the size of a toddler. It's one of the few animals skilled enough to take down a porcupine. It does this most often by repeatedly biting the porcupine on its unprotected face, until the porcu-

pine is weak enough that the fisher can flip it over and attack its
vulnerable belly.

THE WILD TURKEY RESURRECTION

Wild turkeys vanished from New York by the mid-1800s but
were successfully reintroduced in the 1950s. Today, more than
180,000 roam the state. They can run up to 25 mph (40 km/h),
as fast as a bicycle, and fly in short bursts at 55 mph (89 km/h),
almost highway speed.

SHARKS IN NEW YORK WATERS

Believe it or not, New York's coastline is home to more than 25
shark species, ranging from sandbar and dusky sharks to sleek
makos and even great whites. Long Island's waters serve as an
important summer feeding ground, and scientists recently
discovered a nursery for baby great white sharks just offshore.

While sightings have increased as shark populations rebound,
actual attacks on humans are extremely rare. Most of these
ocean predators prefer fish, not people. Their return is seen as a
sign of cleaner waters and healthier marine ecosystems.

A GREAT WHITE NURSERY OFF LONG ISLAND

Marine researchers tagged a young great white shark nicknamed "Liberty" near New York City, confirming that the
waters off Long Island act as a nursery for these iconic predators. Juvenile great whites spend their early months close to
shore, where food is plentiful and larger sharks are less likely to
hunt them. This discovery highlights how New York's coastal
waters play a critical role in the life cycle of one of the ocean's
most famous species.

JAWS AND NEW YORK MYTHS

Jaws, the iconic 1975 shark thriller, was set on the fictional Amity Island, which was implied to be off the coast of New York. But in reality, the movie was filmed on Martha's Vineyard in Massachusetts. Still, the story sparked decades of shark fear along the entire Northeast coast, including Long Island's very real shark habitats.

BIRDS & MIGRATION

THE MIGRATORY SPECTACLE

New York sits along the Atlantic Flyway, a major migratory route used by millions of birds each spring and fall. Sites like Jamaica Bay Wildlife Refuge in Queens host over 330 bird species annually, while Derby Hill on Lake Ontario can record over 40,000 raptors during a single migration season. These natural events draw birdwatchers from around the world and serve as vital stopover points for birds refueling on long journeys.

THE RETURN OF THE BALD EAGLE

In 1976, New York had just one active bald eagle nest. Now, thanks to conservation efforts, the state has over 400 nesting pairs. With wingspans reaching 7.5 feet (2.3 m), about the width of a large SUV, these majestic birds are often spotted along rivers and lakes.

THE PEREGRINE'S PLUNGE

The peregrine falcon population has rebounded in New York. These keen bird killers are thriving in cities, including New

York City, where they nest on bridges and skyscrapers. During hunting dives, they can reach speeds of over 240 mph (386 km/h), fast enough to outrun a Formula One race car.

***

DID YOU KNOW?

Each spring, dozens of migrating songbirds crash into the glass windows of Manhattan skyscrapers—so much so that volunteers now patrol early mornings to rescue stunned birds.

***

REPTILES & AMPHIBIANS

THE HELLBENDER: NEW YORK'S GIANT SALAMANDER

The Eastern hellbender is North America's largest salamander, reaching lengths of over 24 inches (61 cm), about the size of a skateboard. These aquatic amphibians breathe through folds of skin and require clean, fast-moving streams to survive. Nicknamed "snot otters" for their slimy appearance, they now occupy less than 40% of their historic New York range due to pollution and habitat loss.

THE TIMBER RATTLESNAKE: MISUNDERSTOOD NATIVE

New York's largest venomous snake, the timber rattlesnake, can grow over 5 feet (1.5 m) long, roughly the height of a refrigerator. Though fearsome in appearance, these snakes are generally shy and avoid humans. They're listed as threatened in New York and gather each winter in communal dens called hibernacula, where dozens of snakes hibernate together.

THE HIBERNATION MARVEL: BLACKSNAKES

Eastern rat snakes, often called blacksnakes, can hibernate for up to 7 months in New York's cold climate. In winter, they share dens with other species like copperheads and rattlesnakes, peacefully coexisting despite being natural enemies during warmer months.

SPRING PEEPER CHORUS

Tiny spring peeper frogs signal the start of spring with their piercing calls. Though only about 1 inch (2.5 cm) long, roughly the size of a paperclip, they can reach 90 decibels, as loud as a lawn mower. Their choruses begin in late March in southern New York and move north with warming temperatures.

RARE & ENDANGERED WILDLIFE

THE RARE KARNER BLUE

The Karner blue butterfly, named after a hamlet near Albany, is now federally endangered. These tiny butterflies, no bigger than a quarter, depend entirely on wild blue lupine, a plant that has vanished from much of its native habitat. Today, they survive in just a few places, such as the Albany Pine Bush, and are part of active restoration and captive breeding efforts.

THE ELUSIVE MARTEN

The American marten was once wiped out from New York due to trapping and deforestation. This weasel-like forest predator was reintroduced to the Adirondack Mountains in the 1980s and now relies on deep, snowy forests to thrive.

About the size of a small house cat, martens are agile climbers and fierce hunters that spend much of their time in trees. But climate change and habitat fragmentation threaten their long-term survival.

A SECOND CHANCE FOR THE STURGEON

Lake sturgeon are living fossils, massive fish that can live over 100 years and grow up to 7 feet (2.1 m) long, about the length of a dining table. They've survived virtually unchanged for millions of years, with armor-like plates and cartilage skeletons. Nearly wiped out in the early 1900s, sturgeon are now slowly recovering in the Great Lakes and Hudson River thanks to protections and restocking programs.

URBAN WILDLIFE

RACCOONS IN THE ROOFTOPS

Raccoons are highly adaptable and have become common throughout New York City, especially in outer boroughs like Brooklyn and Staten Island. They often nest in chimneys, attics, and even rooftop gardens. Their nimble paws can open latches, zippers, and garbage cans with preposterous precision.

THE INFAMOUS NEW YORK CITY RAT

The brown rat is New York City's most notorious urban animal, with an estimated population of about 3 million. Also known as Norway rats, these resilient rodents can fall from 50 feet (15 m) without injury, tread water for up to 3 days, and squeeze through holes the size of a quarter. Contrary to legend, rats do not outnumber humans in NYC—but they're catching up!

REMARKABLE RAT ABILITIES

New York rats have adapted to urban life in extraordinary ways. Genetic studies show they're distinct from rural rats, with traits that help them survive on human food waste and resist common poisons. A single pair can theoretically produce over 15,000 descendants in one year.

THE GREAT RAT WAR

New York's battle with rats stretches back to colonial times. In the 1990s, the city even had an official "Rat Czar," and today, building managers attend "Rat Academy" workshops to learn modern pest control strategies. Some subway stations have become legendary for their rodent residents.

DID YOU KNOW?

Rats have been filmed dragging entire slices of pizza, bagels, and even a full burrito through New York City subway stations. "Pizza Rat," which was filmed lifting a slice up a staircase, became a viral celebrity in 2015, and is still celebrated as a symbol of NYC's gritty survival spirit.

PETS IN NEW YORK

From pampered pooches in Manhattan high-rises to barn cats and backyard chickens in rural towns, pets are an important part of life all across New York State.

THE WESTMINSTER DOG SHOW

Every February, New York City hosts the world-famous Westminster Kennel Club Dog Show, one of the oldest and most prestigious canine competitions. Held at Madison Square Garden, it attracts thousands of pampered pups, professional handlers, and dog lovers from around the globe.

SUBWAY PUPS AND PET RULES

Subway pup in a handbag. Photo by Renting C
on Unsplash

In New York City, pets are allowed on the subway, but only if they fit in a bag or carrier. Creative New Yorkers have been spotted carrying large dogs in giant tote bags or even Ikea bags with holes cut out for their legs, proving that where there's a will, there's a way.

FAMOUS FELINES OF NEW YORK

The state has its fair share of celebrity cats. Brooklyn once had a bodega cat named Bobo who gained internet fame for lounging on store shelves and greeting customers. And in Albany, a cat named Erastus once served as the unofficial "mayor" of the city's Capitol building, charming lawmakers and visitors alike.

NEW YORK'S FIRST PET CEMETERY

The world's first pet cemetery was established in Hartsdale, New York, in 1896. Today, Hartsdale Pet Cemetery is the resting place of more than 80,000 beloved pets, from dogs and cats to a lion that once belonged to a traveling circus. It even has a War Dog Memorial honoring canines who served in World War I.

DID YOU KNOW?

In New York State, there are more registered dogs than there are people in several small towns. In fact, in some Adirondack communities, it's not unusual for dog licenses to outnumber human residents—especially in off-season months. One tiny town even had a dog elected as honorary mayor!

7

NEW YORK'S TREES AND PLANTS

The Empire State is more than apples and autumn leaves. From ancient forests and wild orchids to carnivorous plants and popcorn-popping cattails, New York's plant life is as diverse and dramatic as its landscapes. Whether you're hiking in the Adirondacks or picking berries in Brooklyn, here's a look at the state's leafy legends and botanical oddities.

ICONIC STATE SYMBOLS

NEW YORK'S STATE TREE: THE SUGAR MAPLE
Designated in 1956, the sugar maple can grow up to 115 feet (35 m) tall, about the height of a 10-story building, and live more than 400 years. Its stunning fall colors are one of New York's most beloved sights. New York is the second-largest maple syrup producer in the U.S., tapping over 800,000 gallons annually. It takes 40 gallons (150 liters) of sap to make just one gallon (3.8 liters) of syrup!

NEW YORK'S STATE FLOWER: THE ROSE
Adopted in 1955, New York's state flower is simply "the rose," with no variety specified. This one-size-fits-all designation allows every rose, from native swamp roses to classic garden hybrids, to stand for the Empire State. It's a fitting floral symbol for such a culturally diverse place.

FRUITS OF NEW YORK

NEW YORK'S APPLE EMPIRE

New York ranks second in the U.S. for apple production, behind Washington, harvesting over 29 million bushels of apples each year (about 42 pounds / 19 kg per bushel) across 55,000 acres (22,000 hectares) of orchards. Popular varieties like Empire, McIntosh, and Cortland thrive in the state's crisp climate.

Cornell University plays a key role because it is New York's land-grant university, meaning it was established to support agriculture and applied science. Through its apple breeding and research programs, Cornell has developed new varieties such as SnapDragon and RubyFrost, designed specifically to grow well in New York's climate and resist common diseases.

THE WILD APPLE FORESTS

Thanks to abandoned orchards from the 1800s, New York has the highest wild apple diversity in the country. These "feral" trees are genetic goldmines, preserving natural resistance to disease, drought, and pests. Cornell University even maintains wild apple preserves to protect this living botanical archive.

GRAPE EXPECTATIONS

New York's Finger Lakes region is one of the top wine-producing areas in the United States. The region's deep, glacial lakes help moderate temperatures, creating perfect conditions for vineyards. Over 1,600 family-run vineyards grow cold-hardy grapes like Concord, Niagara, and Riesling, many of which were first developed in New York.

THE GRAPE THAT STARTED IT ALL

Catawba grapes were once the most widely planted variety in the country. Their pinkish-red hue and tangy flavor made them a hit with early American winemakers. In the mid-1800s, poet Henry Wadsworth Longfellow even wrote a poem celebrating the humble Catawba, helping to popularize it beyond the vineyard.

A FIZZLING LEGACY

In the 1860s, winemaker Nicholas Longworth used Catawba grapes to craft America's first sparkling wines. His champagne-style bubbly was so well regarded that it was said to rival French imports. By the time of the Civil War, he was selling millions of bottles.

DID YOU KNOW?

In 1853, New York's Cayuga Lake region became the first place in the U.S. to sell wine labeled by grape variety—in this case Catawba.

THE BERRY BOUNTY

New York's varied climate supports juicy strawberries, blueberries, raspberries, and blackberries. Many are grown on small family farms in the Hudson Valley, where berry-picking festivals fill the summer calendar.

CHERRIES OF THE NORTH

Northern and western New York produce tart cherries perfect for baking, jam, and juice. While Michigan dominates national cherry production, the Finger Lakes region is famous for its cherry wines and roadside fruit stands that pop up in early summer.

PEACHES IN THE EMPIRE STATE

Despite being better known for apples, New York also grows peaches—especially in its southern tier and along Lake Ontario. The lake helps buffer harsh winter temperatures, allowing peach orchards to survive and flourish. The state's late-summer peaches are known for being exceptionally sweet and juicy.

ANCIENT & UNUSUAL FORESTS

THE ADIRONDACK WHITE PINE GIANTS

Misty morning on Twitchell Lake showing Virgin White Pines in the Adirondack Forest Preserve. Photo via Anne LaBastille, Public domain, via Wikimedia Commons

Eastern white pines once dominated New York's forests, with

the tallest trees reaching an estimated 200–220 feet (61–67 m) —about the height of a 20-story building—according to historical forestry records and early survey accounts. Some exceptional giants grew more than 30 feet (9 m) in circumference, making them among the largest trees ever recorded in eastern North America.

Because these trees were ideal for tall, straight ship masts, the British Crown claimed the largest white pines for the Royal Navy, marking them with a distinctive "Broad Arrow." This symbol meant the trees were legally reserved for naval use and could not be cut by colonists.

While white pines still grow in New York today, the towering old-growth giants that once dominated the forests are now exceedingly rare.

During the American Revolution, leaders such as George Washington also sought white pine timber for ships and military needs. Many trees were so massive that teams of oxen were required just to haul them out of the forest.

ANCIENT FOREST SURVIVORS

In Zoar Valley near Buffalo, tulip poplars and white ash trees soar 150 feet (46 m), as tall as a 14-story building, and some are over 400 years old. The "Wizard of Oz Wood" in the Finger Lakes is home to knotted, untouched trees dating back five centuries.

THE ADIRONDACK WITCH HOBBLE

Nicknamed "witch hobble," this low-growing shrub sends out looping branches that root wherever they touch the ground—creating natural tripwires that can snag unsuspecting hikers. Its fuzzy, mitten-like leaf buds offer frost protection without scales, an unusual trait for northern plants.

CENTRAL PARK'S AMERICAN ELMS

Central Park during Stella snowstorm March 2017. Photo via Emanuel Hahn hahnbo, CC0, via Wikimedia Commons

Central Park protects one of the nation's largest stands of mature American elms—about 1,200 trees in total. "The Mall," also known as Literary Walk, features a soaring canopy of elms planted in the 1860s, forming a green cathedral above one of the park's most iconic walkways.

RARE & EXTREME PLANT LIFE

THE MYSTERIOUS ALBANY PINE BUSH

This 3,300-acre (1,335-hectare) preserve protects one of the world's rare inland pine barrens. Formed by glacial sand dunes, it hosts more than 1,500 species, including the endangered Karner blue butterfly, which survives only where wild blue lupine grows.

DWARF PINE PLAINS

Along the Shawangunk Ridge, pitch pines have adapted to extreme weather and poor soil by growing no taller than 6 feet (1.8 m), even after decades. These pygmy pine plains are among the rarest ecosystems in the state.

NEW YORK'S NATIVE CARNIVORES

New York is home to 14 species of carnivorous plants. The aquatic bladderwort catches tiny water creatures with vacuum-powered traps that snap shut in just 1/50th of a second—making it one of the fastest plants on Earth.

THE ORCHID STATE

New York supports 58 native orchid species. The rarest of all, the ram's head lady's slipper, blooms for just a few days each May and grows in fewer than 10 locations statewide—making it a prize for patient botanists.

DID YOU KNOW?

Foxfire is a soft, blue-green glow produced by bioluminescent fungi found on rotting logs in the woods. On warm, damp nights, it can be bright enough to read by—and early settlers once used it as a natural lantern!

AGRICULTURAL ODDITIES

THE BLACK DIRT REGION

Orange County's "Black Dirt Region" sits atop ancient glacial lakebeds filled with decaying plant matter up to 30 feet (9 m) deep. This ultra-rich soil occasionally caught fire underground in the 1800s and still produces some of the state's best onions and leafy greens.

THE WETLAND WONDERS

Montezuma Wetlands, stretching across 50,000 acres (20,200 hectares) near Cayuga Lake, is one of New York's most important bird habitats. Visitors can spot over 240 bird species while exploring cattail marshes, swamp forests, and elevated boardwalks.

CATTAIL CONFETTI

In New York's wetlands, cattail flowers aren't just decorative—they can put on a dramatic show. When the temperature shifts quickly, especially from warm to cold or during dry spells, the densely packed flower spikes can suddenly burst open, releasing thousands of tiny, fluffy seeds in a soft explosion.

This spontaneous puff is sometimes compared to popcorn popping or a nature-made confetti cannon. The seeds catch the wind and float across the marsh, helping cattails colonize new areas. It's a surprising and strangely satisfying sight for anyone lucky enough to witness it!

THE POISON IVY SHAPESHIFTER

Poison ivy might just be New York's most misunderstood plant —and one of its most adaptable. In the forests of the Adirondacks, it grows as a low shrub. In New York City, it climbs trees, fences, and walls as a woody vine. But the strangest twist? In urban areas, poison ivy produces more potent urushiol—the oil that causes those infamous itchy rashes.

Scientists think higher levels of carbon dioxide in cities may be supercharging the plant's oil production. So while it might be hiding in plain sight, this shapeshifter packs a more powerful punch in the concrete jungle than in the wilderness.

DID YOU KNOW?

American ginseng, introduced to European settlers by Native Americans, became New York's first major export crop to China in the 1700s. A single dried wild root can sell for hundreds of dollars. "Sang hunting" remains a seasonal tradition in the Adirondacks, but it's closely monitored to prevent over-harvesting.

8

NEW YORK'S PEOPLE AND POPULATION

Nearly 20 million people call New York home—but no two corners of the state look the same. From the crowds of Manhattan to quiet mountain hamlets, this is a place of extremes, contrasts, and constant change. It's a state shaped by waves of immigrants, Indigenous traditions, deep cultural enclaves, and billion-dollar paychecks right alongside small-town life. Here's a closer look at the people who make New York, well...New York.

POPULATION STATISTICS

FOURTH MOST POPULOUS STATE

As of 2024, New York's population is estimated at around 19.87 million people, making it the fourth most populous state in the U.S., behind only California, Texas, and Florida. Although its growth slowed in recent decades, the state has recently seen a rebound after pandemic-era declines.

ONE CITY, 43% OF THE STATE'S POPULATION

New York City is home to approximately 8.48 million people—nearly 43% of New York State's total population. The larger New York metropolitan area, which includes parts of New Jersey and Connecticut, is the largest metropolitan area in the United States, with about 20 million residents.

DID YOU KNOW?

If New York City were its own state, it would rank as the 12th most populous in the U.S.—larger than states like Virginia and Colorado, and more populated than 38 other individual states combined.

TINY TOWN IN THE MOUNTAINS

The hamlet of Adirondack in Essex County has just 86 year-round residents, making it one of the smallest incorporated communities in the state. During the summer, that number swells dramatically as tourists and seasonal residents arrive in the scenic Adirondacks.

EXTREMES OF SPRAWL AND SPARSITY

New York State showcases a dramatic urban-rural divide. Manhattan is one of the most densely populated places in the country, with over 72,000 people per square mile (27,800 per km^2), while Hamilton County in the Adirondacks averages just 2.8 people per square mile (1.1 per km^2), the lowest population density of any county east of the Mississippi River.

PEOPLE WHO LIVE IN THE PARK

Adirondack Park is the only major state park in the United States where people live year-round. About 132,000 people call it home, with a median age of 47—eight years older than the state average. Over 20% of homes in the park are seasonal, which means small towns often triple in population during the summer.

RETIREMENT HAVEN BY THE SEA

The town of Southold, on Long Island's North Fork, has the oldest population in the state, with a median age of 60.1 years. With its vineyards, beaches, and small-town charm, Southold has become a magnet for retirees. Nearly 40% of its residents are over age 65.

THE YOUNGEST TOWN IN AMERICA

In stark contrast, the village of Kiryas Joel in Orange County has a median age of just 15.1 years, making it the youngest town in the entire country. This Hasidic Jewish community has the highest fertility rate in the U.S., with families averaging nearly six children and over half the population is under 18.

ECONOMIC DEMOGRAPHICS

A STATE FULL OF MILLIONAIRES

New York is home to around 1.1 million millionaire households, meaning households with a net worth of at least $1 million. That represents roughly 14–15% of all households statewide, or about 1 in every 7.

New York consistently ranks second in the United States for both the number of millionaire households and the number of billionaires, behind California, which holds the top spot in each category.

HOME TO HUNDREDS OF BILLIONAIRES

New York State is home to around 140 billionaires, placing it among the top-ranked states in the country for extreme wealth.

The majority live in New York City, which consistently ranks as one of the world's leading hubs for billionaires.

This extraordinary concentration of wealth exists alongside some of the nation's highest poverty rates, highlighting the sharp economic contrasts found across the state.

A STAGGERING INCOME GAP

New York has some of the greatest income inequality in the United States. In Nassau County, New York, the median household income is about $120,000 USD, far above the U.S. median of roughly $75,000. Meanwhile, in The Bronx, that figure drops to about $41,000, roughly half the statewide average.

WALL STREET'S IMPACT

The financial industry plays a massive role in New York's economy. In 2023, Wall Street bonuses alone totaled $33.7 billion USD. The securities industry—companies that trade and manage investments such as stocks and bonds—accounts for about one-fifth of all private-sector wages in New York City, despite employing less than 5% of the workforce.

THE RURAL ECONOMIC STRUGGLE

While Wall Street thrives, many rural areas of New York face economic hardship. In counties like St. Lawrence and Steuben, median household incomes can dip below $55,000 USD. In some places, over 1 in 5 residents live below the poverty line.

THE RISING TECH SECTOR

New York's tech workforce has grown rapidly, especially in Manhattan, Brooklyn, and the Capital Region's Tech Valley. Big names like Google, Meta, and Amazon have built major offices, while homegrown companies like Etsy and Datadog are thriving. Together, these firms are fueling job growth and helping to diversify an economy once centered on finance and manufacturing.

HOUSING AFFORDABILITY CHALLENGES

Despite its economic power, New York struggles with housing affordability. The median home price in NYC exceeds $700,000 USD, pricing many out of the market and increasing demand for rental housing. This contributes to homelessness and displacement issues, especially in lower-income neighborhoods.

ECONOMIC MOBILITY—A MIXED BAG

New York offers some of the best and worst opportunities for economic mobility. While NYC provides access to high-paying industries, expensive housing and childcare make it hard for low-income families to get ahead. Meanwhile, smaller cities like Syracuse and Utica often offer cheaper living—but fewer high-wage jobs.

DID YOU KNOW?

New York's wealthiest zip code isn't in Manhattan—it's 11962 in Sagaponack, a tiny Long Island hamlet in the Hamptons. With just a few hundred full-time residents, the median home price is over $5 million USD. Some houses are so large, they include indoor pools, wine cellars, and private theaters!

THE FIRST NEW YORKERS: INDIGENOUS PEOPLES AND NATIONS

NEW YORK'S ORIGINAL INHABITANTS

Long before European settlers arrived, the land now known as New York was home to thriving Indigenous nations. The Haudenosaunee Confederacy (also known as the Iroquois) united the Mohawk, Oneida, Onondaga, Cayuga, and Seneca peoples—and later the Tuscarora—into one of the most sophisticated political alliances in North America. Formed more than 800 years ago, it established a system of governance that influenced later democratic ideas.

These nations lived primarily in what is now upstate New York. Meanwhile, Algonquian-speaking peoples such as the Lenape and Mahican lived along the Hudson River and coastal areas, with rich cultural traditions and deep ties to the land.

NATIVE NEW YORKERS TODAY

Today, about 194,000 people in New York State identify as having Native American heritage, making up less than 1% of the population. The state officially recognizes nine Native nations, with the largest reservation being the St. Regis Mohawk Reservation (Akwesasne) in northern Franklin County, which crosses into Canada.

New York City is home to the largest urban Native American population in the northeastern U.S., with around 27,000 residents representing tribes from all over North America.

THE SHINNECOCK NATION'S UNIQUE STATUS

The Shinnecock Indian Nation, based on eastern Long Island,

gained federal recognition in 2010 after a legal fight that lasted more than 30 years. But their roots in the region go back thousands of years, with archaeological evidence confirming a continuous presence. Today, their 800-acre reservation sits amid some of the most expensive real estate in the country, creating a striking contrast between tribal lands and the nearby luxury homes of the Hamptons.

THE SENECA NATION'S ECONOMIC INFLUENCE

The Seneca Nation is a major economic force in western New York. It operates three successful casinos that generate over one billion dollars each year, funding tribal healthcare, education, and other services. The Seneca Nation also owns commercial property in Buffalo and Niagara Falls, giving it a strong presence in some of the region's biggest cities.

NATIVE COMMUNITIES IN THE ADIRONDACKS

The Akwesasne Mohawk community, also known as the St. Regis Mohawk Reservation, spans the U.S.–Canada border in northern Franklin County.

In some parts of the county, Native Americans make up the majority of the population—something rare in the eastern United States. Akwesasne has its own police force, schools, and cultural institutions, and tribal members regularly cross the international border, reflecting their sovereign status within New York State.

THE "KEEPERS OF THE EASTERN DOOR"

The Mohawk Nation is known as the "Keepers of the Eastern Door" because they were the easternmost nation in the Haudenosaunee Confederacy. Their territory acted as the first line of defense against threats from the east, making them key protectors of the Confederacy's lands and people.

THE HAUDENOSAUNNEE CONFEDERACY GOVERNANCE

The Haudenosaunee Confederacy created one of the world's oldest participatory democracies. Their Great Law of Peace outlined a system of government with checks and balances and a shared council, while still allowing each nation to govern itself. These principles helped inspire elements of the U.S. Constitution, including federalism and representative government.

THE TWO ROW WAMPUM TREATY

The Two Row Wampum is one of the oldest treaty agreements between Indigenous peoples and European settlers in North America.

Created around 1613 between the Haudenosaunee and Dutch traders, the wampum belt features two parallel rows of purple beads on a white background. These two rows represent a European ship and a Haudenosaunee canoe traveling the same river side by side—each steering their own vessel, respecting one another's path, and not interfering in each other's way of life.

This agreement established a relationship based on mutual respect, peace, and non-interference. For many Indigenous nations, the Two Row Wampum still serves as a living symbol of how nations can coexist with sovereignty and dignity.

IMMIGRATION AND DIVERSITY

NEW YORK'S DIVERSE POPULATION

New York is one of the most diverse states in the country. Around 44% of residents identify as non-Hispanic white, 19% as Hispanic or Latino, 17% as Black or African American, and 9% as Asian, with the remainder identifying as mixed race or other ethnicities. More than 200 languages are spoken across the state, and nearly 30% of New Yorkers speak a language other than English at home.

ELLIS ISLAND LEGACY

From 1892 to 1954, Ellis Island in New York Harbor was the main entry point for immigrants arriving in the United States. More than 12 million people passed through its gates. On its busiest day in 1907, nearly 12,000 newcomers were processed. Today, about 40% of New Yorkers are either immigrants themselves or the children of immigrants—one of the highest proportions in the country.

ELLIS ISLAND: ISLAND OF HOPE AND TEARS

Ellis Island is often called the "Island of Hope and Tears." For many, it represented the chance to start a new life in America. But for some, it meant separation, waiting, and heartbreak.

Roughly 2% of arrivals were turned away due to failed medical exams, missing paperwork, or other disqualifications. Immigrants could be held in crowded dormitories for days or even weeks, often uncertain if they would be allowed to stay or reunited with their families. Still, for millions, Ellis Island stood as a powerful symbol of hope and possibility.

THE FASTEST-GROWING ETHNIC GROUP

Asian Americans are the fastest-growing major ethnic group in New York, with the population increasing by nearly 38% between 2010 and 2020. Queens is now home to the most diverse Asian American community in the country, with large numbers of residents from China, India, Korea, the Philippines, Bangladesh, and Pakistan. The neighborhood of Flushing has become the city's largest Chinatown, filled with restaurants, shops, and street life that reflect cultures from across Asia.

THE EXODUS AND RETURN

During the COVID-19 pandemic, New York saw a major population dip as about 350,000 people left the state in 2020. But by 2022 and 2023, many began returning—especially to New York City. Manhattan saw a rise in apartment rentals and subway ridership again, showing that the city's energy and pull hadn't disappeared for good.

UPSTATE POPULATION CHALLENGES

While the New York City area has bounced back, many upstate communities—regions north and west of New York City—are still shrinking. Since 2010, about 40 of New York's 62 counties have lost population, particularly in the Southern Tier, a region along New York's southern border with Pennsylvania, and in Western New York.

Cities such as Jamestown, New York and Elmira, New York have lost 10% or more of their population since 2000, often linked to fewer job opportunities and younger residents moving elsewhere. For many small towns, attracting new residents has become a top priority.

DID YOU KNOW?

Some upstate New York towns are offering cash incentives, tax breaks, or even free land to attract new residents and remote workers. Places like Buffalo, Rochester, and small towns in the Catskills and Mohawk Valley have launched programs to help revitalize their communities—offering everything from relocation grants to co-working space discounts. It's all part of a creative push to bring new life (and new people) to shrinking areas.

CULTURAL ENCLAVES

THE "LITTLE ITALY" LEGACY

Manhattan's Little Italy may have gotten smaller over the years, but Italian American culture remains strong across New York State. In the Bronx, the Belmont neighborhood—often called the "real Little Italy"—is home to multi-generational families, old-school bakeries, and classic Italian markets. Nearly 14% of New Yorkers claim Italian ancestry, making it the largest Italian American population in the country.

THE POLISH ENCLAVE OF GREENPOINT

Greenpoint, Brooklyn, is home to one of the largest Polish American communities in the United States, second only to Chicago. Polish bakeries, Catholic churches, and bilingual shop signs line the neighborhood's streets. During the Cold War, Greenpoint became a center of support for Polish independence movements, including the Solidarity labor movement that helped bring down communism in Poland.

Even the nearby Kosciuszko Bridge (pronounced *kah-SHOOSH-koh*) honors Polish heritage. The bridge, which carries the Brooklyn-Queens Expressway across Newtown Creek, is named after Tadeusz Kościuszko, a Polish military engineer who fought alongside George Washington during the American Revolution.

BRIGHTON BEACH: "LITTLE ODESSA BY THE SEA"

Brighton Beach, located along the southern Brooklyn coast, has one of the largest Russian-speaking communities outside Russia. It became a hub for Soviet Jewish refugees in the 1970s and still reflects the culture and language of that era.

Today, the neighborhood is home to people from across the former USSR, including Ukraine, Belarus, Georgia, and Central Asia, making it one of the most unique cultural enclaves in the city.

THE SIKH ENCLAVE OF RICHMOND HILL

Richmond Hill in Queens—often called Little Punjab—is home to one of the largest Sikh communities outside India. The neighborhood features multiple gurdwaras (Sikh temples). Each April, the annual Sikh Day Parade brings vibrant colors, music, and tens of thousands of participants to the streets of Manhattan in celebration of Sikh identity and unity.

THE GARIFUNA COMMUNITY

The South Bronx is home to the largest Garifuna population in the United States, with around 200,000 people from Honduras, Belize, Guatemala, and Nicaragua. The Garifuna are an Afro-Indigenous group with a rich cultural heritage that blends African, Caribbean, and Indigenous traditions.

They preserve their unique language—called Garifuna—which was recognized in 2001 by UNESCO as a Masterpiece of the Oral and Intangible Heritage of Humanity. Music and dance remain central to their identity, especially lively punta rhythms and festive jankunu performances.

NEW YORK'S MARITIME ISLAND

Tucked away in the Bronx, City Island feels more like a New England fishing village than part of New York City. Just 1.5 miles long, the island has about 4,500 residents and a strong seafaring history.

Families here have built boats for generations, and in the early 1900s, local shipyards produced yachts that went on to win the America's Cup. Today, the island is known for its seafood shacks, sailing culture, and laid-back charm.

THE BUKHARIAN JEWISH ENCLAVE

Forest Hills and Rego Park in Queens are home to the largest Bukharian Jewish community outside Israel, with an estimated 50,000 to 60,000 residents. Originally from Uzbekistan and Tajikistan, Bukharian Jews have preserved their unique traditions, music, food, and religious practices for over 2,000 years. They speak Bukhori, a dialect of Persian that has been passed down across centuries and continents.

Today, Queens is filled with Bukharian synagogues, schools, and businesses that keep this ancient culture alive.

THE DOMINICAN HEARTLAND

Washington Heights in Upper Manhattan is often called "Little Dominican Republic." With more than 160,000 Dominican residents, it is the largest Dominican community outside the Caribbean nation. The neighborhood is a hub of Dominican culture, featuring lively street festivals, restaurants serving plantain-based dishes like mofongo and mangú, and local politicians who maintain close ties to the Dominican Republic. The neighborhood's Caribbean spirit is felt on nearly every corner.

DID YOU KNOW?

New York State has more diplomatic missions than anywhere else in the U.S. outside of Washington, D.C. In addition to the United Nations headquarters in Manhattan, dozens of countries maintain embassies, consulates, and official residences across the state.

These properties operate under special international agreements—meaning they're technically foreign territory. Some diplomatic buildings are hidden in plain sight, and they are located not only in major cities but also in quiet suburbs and even small upstate towns.

LGBTQ+ COMMUNITIES AND HISTORY

BIRTHPLACE OF THE MODERN LGBTQ+ MOVEMENT

The Stonewall Inn in Manhattan's Greenwich Village was the site of the 1969 Stonewall Uprising, widely considered the spark for the modern LGBTQ+ rights movement. When police raided the bar on June 28, 1969, patrons—led by transgender women of color like Marsha P. Johnson and Sylvia Rivera—resisted, igniting several nights of protests.

This powerful act of defiance is honored every year through Pride events around the world. In 2016, President Barack Obama designated the Stonewall Inn and its surrounding area as the first U.S. national monument dedicated to LGBTQ+ history.

AMERICA'S FIRST TRANSGENDER COMMUNITY

In the 1950s and 60s, a small rural retreat in the Catskills became one of the earliest known transgender communities in America. Called Casa Susanna, it offered transgender women a rare safe space to live openly and build friendships during a time when public expression was often criminalized.

This hidden chapter of history was uncovered decades later through a collection of photographs found at a flea market, inspiring both a Broadway play and a documentary that brought Casa Susanna's legacy into the spotlight.

VOGUING AND BALLROOM CULTURE

Voguing is a striking dance style born out of New York City's Black and Latinx LGBTQ+ ballroom scene in the 1980s. Dancers combine dramatic poses, intricate hand movements, and fierce runway walks to express identity and emotion.

Ballroom culture created inclusive spaces where people facing racism, homophobia, and transphobia could celebrate who they were. While Madonna's 1990 hit Vogue helped introduce the style to the world, voguing and ballroom remain deeply rooted in queer resilience and creativity—and continue to thrive today.

CHELSEA AND HELL'S KITCHEN

Chelsea and Hell's Kitchen in Manhattan are two of New York's most iconic LGBTQ+ neighborhoods. Chelsea rose to prominence in the 1980s as a cultural and social hub, with Hell's Kitchen following close behind. The stretch of 8th Avenue running though was once nicknamed "the catwalk," known as a stylish social promenade and meeting place.

Today, both areas are home to LGBTQ+-owned businesses, arts spaces, and community centers—and have the highest density of same-sex couples in the state.

PARK SLOPE'S "DYKE SLOPE"

In the 1980s and 90s, Brooklyn's Park Slope became known as "Dyke Slope" thanks to its large and visible lesbian community. It was one of the first neighborhoods in the U.S. where same-sex couples raising children became a common and accepted sight. The area was known for its progressive values, with food co-ops, women-owned bookstores and cafes, and alternative schools that reflected the community's inclusive spirit.

LESLIE-LOHMAN MUSEUM OF ART

Located in SoHo, the Leslie-Lohman Museum of Art is the world's first and only museum devoted exclusively to LGBTQ+ art. It began in 1969 as a small gallery created by Charles Leslie and Fritz Lohman, who were determined to preserve works by gay artists at a time when many artworks were discarded, ignored, or lost—especially during the AIDS crisis.

Today, the museum holds over 30,000 pieces and continues to celebrate queer creativity and history through exhibitions, events, and education.

PIONEERING LEGISLATION

New York has often led the way in advancing LGBTQ+ rights. After 15 years of activism, New York City passed its first gay rights bill in 1983. The state followed with the Sexual Orientation Non-Discrimination Act (SONDA) in 2002, protecting LGBTQ+ individuals statewide.

In 2011, New York became the largest state at the time to legalize same-sex marriage—doing so through legislative vote, not a court ruling. Then in 2019, the Gender Expression Non-Discrimination Act (GENDA) passed after more than a decade of advocacy, extending protections for transgender and gender nonconforming people.

THE GROWING DEMOGRAPHICS

As of 2022, about 7.7% of New York adults identify as LGBTQ+—more than double the percentage from just ten years earlier. New York ranks sixth in the nation by percentage and first in total population, with nearly one million LGBTQ+ adults living in the New York City metro area. This large and diverse community supports institutions like the Lesbian Herstory Archives in Brooklyn and the Audre Lorde Project, which focuses on the needs of LGBTQ+ people of color.

NEW YORK'S WELCOME MAT

New York is consistently ranked among the most LGBTQ+-friendly states in the country. It has passed wide-ranging protections, including bans on conversion therapy for minors, simplified gender marker changes, and requirements for LGBTQ+-inclusive education in public schools.

New York was the first state to prohibit discrimination against transgender patients, and requires insurance coverage for gender-affirming care. In 2022, it launched the Office of LGBTQ+ Affairs—one of the few state-level offices in the nation dedicated to supporting queer and trans communities across government programs.

RELIGIOUS AND SPIRITUAL COMMUNITIES

JEWISH NEW YORK

New York is home to the largest Jewish population in the United States, with more than 1.7 million Jewish residents statewide. About 1.3 million of them live in New York City, giving the city the largest Jewish population of any city in the world outside Israel.

Brooklyn alone is home to roughly 500,000 Jewish residents, making it the largest Jewish community of any borough or county in the United States. The population includes a wide range of Hasidic, Orthodox, Conservative, and Reform communities. From kosher markets to synagogues and schools, Jewish life remains a central part of New York's cultural fabric.

HASIDIC COMMUNITIES

The town of Ramapo in Rockland County has the highest concentration of Hasidic Jews outside Israel. Within it lies the village of New Square, one of the few theocratic communities in the United States. Founded in 1954 by members of the Skverer Hasidic movement, the village was designed as a religious enclave and continues to follow the guidance of its spiritual leader. Today, more than 98% of New Square's residents are part of the Hasidic community.

THE YIDDISH PRESS SURVIVAL

New York City remains a global center for Yiddish-language publishing, despite predictions that the language would fade away. Hasidic neighborhoods in Brooklyn, like Williamsburg and Borough Park, support several Yiddish newspapers, including Der Yid, Der Blatt, and Di Tzeitung. In many of these communities, children grow up speaking Yiddish at home and only begin learning English once they start school, keeping the language very much alive.

THE SHAKER LEGACY

Although the Shaker movement is no longer active, its legacy lives on in New York State. The Shakers were known for their devotion to simplicity, celibacy, pacifism, and exquisite craftsmanship. One of their most important settlements, Mount Lebanon Shaker Village in New Lebanon, has been preserved as a historic site.

Visitors can explore original buildings, view artifacts, and learn about this distinctive religious community's influence on American culture and design.

THE SENECA NATION'S SPIRITUAL TRADITIONS

The Seneca Nation, one of the six nations of the Haudenosaunee Confederacy, preserves spiritual practices deeply tied to nature and seasonal cycles. Ceremonies include sacred fire rituals, thanksgiving festivals, and longhouse gatherings that continue to play a central role in Seneca community life. These traditions honor the land, the harvest, and the interconnectedness of all living things.

THE SURPRISING AMISH BOOM

New York now has one of the fastest-growing Amish populations in the country. Since 2000, the number of Amish residents has grown by more than 800 percent. Drawn by affordable farmland and rural isolation, Amish families have established dozens of new settlements across upstate New York.

St. Lawrence County now hosts one of the largest Amish communities in the U.S., where horse-drawn buggies, plain dress, and roadside farm stands are increasingly common sights in the North Country.

INTERFAITH COMMUNITIES

New York City is home to one of the most active interfaith networks in the United States. Organizations across the city promote collaboration and understanding among Jewish, Christian, Muslim, Hindu, Sikh, Buddhist, and other spiritual communities.

These interfaith efforts include public forums, service projects, and youth initiatives that foster respect across religious lines in one of the world's most diverse cities.

MEDIUMS AND SPIRITUALISTS

The town of Lily Dale in Chautauqua County has the highest concentration of mediums and spiritualists in the world. Founded in 1879, this small community has around 275 year-round residents, but each summer, more than 22,000 visitors arrive for workshops, lectures, and spiritual readings. Lily Dale operates as a self-governed spiritualist community, complete with its own post office, auditorium, and healing temple.

SPIRITUALISM IN THE HUDSON VALLEY

The Hudson Valley has long been a center for spiritualist movements, but was especially so during the 19th century when interest in séances and spirit communication swept the country.

Mediums and spiritual gatherings drew visitors hoping to reach loved ones from beyond death, and the region remains a hub for metaphysical retreats, holistic healing, and alternative spiritual practices to this day.

CATHOLICISM IN NEW YORK

The Archdiocese of New York is one of the largest Catholic dioceses in the United States, serving millions of Catholics through hundreds of parishes, schools, and charities. At its heart is St. Patrick's Cathedral, an iconic Gothic Revival church in Midtown Manhattan completed in 1878.

It remains a major place of worship, pilgrimage, and architectural wonder for both locals and visitors from around the world.

DID YOU KNOW?

The Cathedral of Saint John the Divine in Manhattan is the largest Anglican cathedral in the world, and its unfinished construction has earned it the nickname "St. John the Unfinished." It serves as a cultural hub, hosting concerts, art exhibits, and interfaith events.

LANGUAGES AND DIALECTS

NEW YORK'S LANGUAGE MOSAIC

New York is one of the most linguistically diverse places on Earth. About 30% of residents speak a language other than English at home, and across the state hundreds of different languages and dialects are spoken. This remarkable mix reflects New York's long history as a global crossroads for immigration.

LANGUAGES IN NEW YORK CITY

Language diversity is especially concentrated in New York City. Linguists estimate that around 200 languages are spoken across the city's five boroughs in daily life, with Queens alone accounting for roughly 160 of them.

In neighborhoods like Jackson Heights, nearly 60% of residents speak a language other than English at home—making a single walk down the street feel like a trip around the world.

LINGUISTIC TREASURES

Beyond widely spoken languages, New York is also a refuge for rare and endangered tongues. Researchers at the Endangered Language Alliance have documented more than 600 distinct languages and dialects in the New York City metropolitan area —more than in any other city worldwide.

Some of these languages are spoken by only a few hundred people globally. In several cases, New York now hosts the largest remaining speaker communities outside their original homelands, making the city an unexpected stronghold for linguistic survival.

CITY OF BABEL

To serve its multilingual residents, New York City provides government services in at least ten major languages—including Spanish, Mandarin, Cantonese, Russian, Bengali, Haitian Creole, Korean, Arabic, Urdu, French, and Polish. During emergencies, important public information is translated into multiple languages to ensure all communities stay informed and safe. In a city where translation is part of daily life, linguistic access isn't just helpful—it's essential.

NEW YORK'S TRANSLATION INFRASTRUCTURE

New York's extraordinary linguistic diversity has created a vast translation and interpretation network. Courts regularly employ interpreters for dozens of languages, ranging from widely spoken ones like Spanish to rare Indigenous languages brought by immigrant and refugee communities, including Mixtec from southern Mexico and Q'anjob'al from Guatemala.

Public schools across the state support students speaking more than 100 different languages, reflecting families who have arrived from nearly every part of the world. Together, these services make New York's language infrastructure among the most comprehensive in the nation.

DISAPPEARING DIALECTS

While New York embraces global languages, some of its classic local speech patterns are fading. Linguists at Columbia and NYU have found that the traditional New York City accent—famous for its dropped R's and stretched vowels—is declining, especially among younger generations and in neighborhoods undergoing gentrification. Brooklyn and Bronx accents still survive in some communities, but like the city itself, they continue to evolve.

THE REMARKABLE DEAF COMMUNITY

The Rochester area has the highest per-capita deaf population in the United States. Around 90,000 people in the region are deaf or hard of hearing, creating a deeply inclusive environment.

Businesses often employ American Sign Language (ASL) interpreters, and Rochester was the first city to develop an emergency dispatch system designed specifically for deaf users. The community even has its own local dialect of ASL, with signs unique to the area.

This strong presence is largely thanks to institutions like the Rochester School for the Deaf and the National Technical Institute for the Deaf, a college within the Rochester Institute of Technology (RIT).

ARABIC-SPEAKING NEW YORK

New York City has the largest Arabic-speaking population in the United States. Brooklyn's Bay Ridge neighborhood is a cultural hub for Arab Americans, filled with bakeries, mosques, bookstores, and markets representing communities from Yemen, Egypt, Palestine, and beyond. Arabic is one of the top 10 most spoken languages in the city—and a vital part of its multicultural identity.

NEW YORK PUBLIC LIBRARIES: A HUB FOR MULTILINGUAL RESOURCES

New York City's public library system is one of the largest in the world, and one of the most linguistically inclusive. Library branches offer books, media, and programming in dozens of languages to reflect the communities they serve.

Many locations host free English classes, citizenship preparation courses, and cultural celebrations. For many immigrant families, the local library is more than a place for books, it's a bridge to language learning, cultural preservation, and connection.

DID YOU KNOW?

New York was one of the first states in the U.S. to mandate multilingual emergency alerts, court interpreters for rare languages, and language access services in schools and hospitals. It's not just about translation—it's about making sure every resident can understand their rights, get help, and feel heard.

9

WORLD RECORD-BREAKING FACTS & STATS

If New York had a trophy case, it would need its own zip code. From waterfalls and subways to skyscrapers and Olympic moments, the Empire State is home to more record-setters than you might expect. Some are official world records, others are jaw-dropping local feats, but all are uniquely New York.

NEW YORK CITY RECORDS

LARGEST SUBWAY SYSTEM BY NUMBER OF STATIONS

With 472 active stations, the New York City Subway has more stops than any other subway system in the world. Before the COVID-19 pandemic, it carried more than 5.5 million riders on a typical weekday. If you stretched all its tracks into one line, they would reach roughly the distance between New York City and Chicago.

CENTRAL PARK: THE WORLD'S MOST PHOTOGRAPHED PARK

Central Park is New York City's backyard—843 acres (341 hectares) of trails, lakes, and open space tucked right into the middle of Manhattan. Every year, about 42 million people visit, which is more people than visit Yellowstone, Yosemite, and the Grand Canyon combined. Although it feels like a patch of wilderness in the city, it was carefully designed by Frederick Law Olmsted and Calvert Vaux to look natural, while offering the perfect setting for strolls, selfies, concerts, and quiet escapes.

LARGEST DEPARTMENT STORE IN THE U.S.

Macy's Herald Square. Photo via Arild Vågen, CC BY-SA 4.0, via Wikimedia Commons

Macy's Herald Square covers an entire city block and offers a staggering 2.5 million square feet (232,000 sq m) of retail space spread across 11 floors. It is the largest department store in the United States and draws more than 20 million shoppers each year.

While it is slightly smaller than the world's largest department store, Shinsegae Centum City in South Korea, Macy's has earned legendary status thanks to its size, its history, its starring role in *Miracle on 34th Street*, and its connection to the annual Macy's Thanksgiving Day Parade, one of the most beloved holiday traditions in America.

TRAIN STATION WITH THE MOST PLATFORMS

When it comes to platforms, Grand Central Terminal is the world's largest train station. The terminal boasts 44 platforms and 67 tracks spread across two underground levels. Grand Central terminal stretches across 48 acres (19 hectares) and welcomes around 750,000 people each day. Its ceiling is decorated with a mural of 2,500 stars, including a few intentionally reversed constellations that continue to fascinate visitors and astronomy fans alike.

THE HIGH LINE: A GLOBAL INSPIRATION

The High Line is a 1.45-mile (2.33 kilometer) elevated park that runs through Manhattan's west side on what used to be an abandoned freight rail line. Though not the world's longest linear park, it has inspired dozens of similar projects in cities around the globe. Since its opening, property values near The High Line have more than doubled, turning a rusty piece of infrastructure into one of New York's most popular green spaces.

WORLD'S LARGEST GOLD REPOSITORY

Hidden deep beneath the streets of Lower Manhattan, the Federal Reserve Bank of New York holds the largest known gold reserve in the world. About 6,700 tons of gold—worth around 365 billion dollars—are stored in a secure vault 80 feet underground. Much of the gold belongs to foreign governments and central banks, making this unassuming downtown building one of the most heavily protected places on Earth.

FASTEST ELEVATORS IN THE WESTERN HEMISPHERE

The elevators at One World Trade Center reach speeds of 23 miles per hour (37 kilom per hour), making them the fastest in the Western Hemisphere. In just 60 seconds, you can travel from the ground to the 102nd floor.

During the ride, visitors can view a floor-to-ceiling animated time-lapse that shows how New York City transformed from marshland to modern skyline. While impressive, these elevators run at nearly half the speed of the world record holder in China's Guangzhou CTF Finance Centre, which hits 45 miles per hour (72 kilom per hour).

WORLD'S LARGEST FINANCIAL CENTER

New York's Financial District is the largest financial hub in the world. At its core is the New York Stock Exchange, which lists companies valued at more than 25 trillion dollars. Just steps away, the famous "Charging Bull" sculpture has become a global symbol of economic strength, optimism, and high-stakes trading.

ONE OF THE LARGEST LIBRARIES IN THE WORLD

The New York Public Library (NYPL) is the largest public library system in the United States and the second-largest library overall, after the Library of Congress. With 92 branches and more than 53 million items, it serves millions of readers across Manhattan, the Bronx, and Staten Island.

One of two marble lions outside The New York Public
Library main branch. Photo by Richard Hedrick on Unsplash

New York City's other two boroughs—Brooklyn and Queens—
operate their own separate public library systems. NYPL's
grand main branch on Fifth Avenue is famously guarded by
two marble lions named Patience and Fortitude.

LARGEST ART MUSEUM IN THE U.S.

The Metropolitan Museum of Art (MET) is home to more
than 2 million works of art spanning 5,000 years. If you spent

just 30 seconds looking at each piece, it would take you over a year to see it all—without breaks! Beyond its world-class galleries, the museum's rooftop garden offers spectacular views of Central Park and hosts seasonal exhibits and events. And those famous front steps? They've starred in everything from fashion shoots to movie scenes.

MOST BRIDGES AND TUNNELS IN THE U.S.

New York City has more bridges and tunnels than any other city in the United States, with 789 bridges and 13 tunnels connecting its five boroughs and surrounding regions. The Brooklyn Bridge, completed in 1883, was a marvel of its time. It was the first steel-wire suspension bridge, and held the record as the longest in the world when it opened.

The bridge's completion was also made possible by Emily Warren Roebling, who stepped in to oversee construction after her husband, chief engineer Washington Roebling, became seriously ill.

OLDEST AND LARGEST ST. PATRICK'S DAY PARADE

New York City's St. Patrick's Day Parade is both the oldest and the largest in the world. It started in 1762, even before the Declaration of Independence, and today draws around 2 million spectators each year. That is about four times the crowd that attends Dublin's celebration, making it one of New York's proudest and greenest traditions.

ONE OF THE WORLD'S MOST VALUABLE SPORTS FRANCHISES

The New York Yankees are not just a legendary baseball team, they are one of the most valuable sports franchises on the planet, worth over 6 billion dollars. The team has won 27 World Series championships, more than any other franchise in Major League Baseball and the most in North American professional sports.

The Yankees' iconic pinstripe uniforms and interlocking "NY" logo have become globally recognized symbols of baseball excellence.

LONGEST-RUNNING BROADWAY SHOW

The Phantom of the Opera enchanted audiences for an incredible 13,925 performances between 1988 and 2023, earning the title of Broadway's longest-running show. While it holds the record in New York, the global title still belongs to London's The Mousetrap, which has been running continuously since 1952 with more than 28,000 performances.

DID YOU KNOW?

The Metropolitan Transportation Authority (MTA) Lost Property Unit in NYC handles over 50,000 lost items every year—from musical instruments to false teeth—and reunites many with their owners.

NEW YORK STATE RECORDS

ADIRONDACK PARK: LARGEST PROTECTED AREA IN THE LOWER 48

Adirondack Park stretches across more than 6.1 million acres (about 2.5 million hectares), making it larger than Yellowstone, Yosemite, Grand Canyon, Glacier, and Great Smoky Mountains National Parks combined.

It covers nearly one-fifth of New York State. Unlike most parks, it's a mix of public and private land, so people actually live within its borders. In some areas, cell service is still hard to come by, and you can hike for days without seeing another person.

ERIE CANAL: A 19TH-CENTURY ENGINEERING MARVEL

When it opened in 1825, the Erie Canal was the second-longest canal in the world and completely transformed trade in America. It reduced shipping costs by 95%, and helped turn New York City into the country's busiest port.

Built mostly by hand with the help of horses and pulleys, it earned the nickname "Clinton's Ditch" after Governor DeWitt Clinton, who championed the project despite fierce opposition. Today, you can bike, walk, or paddle along its scenic route and imagine life during the canal's heyday.

TAUGHANNOCK FALLS: TALLEST SINGLE-DROP WATERFALL EAST OF THE ROCKIES

Taughannock Falls plunges 215 feet (65 m) in a single drop—taller than the American Falls at Niagara and about as high as a 20-story building.

Taughannock Falls. Photo via depositphotos.com

The water cascades into a glacially carved gorge with dramatic cliffs on either side. In winter, the falls can freeze into a spectacular ice column. According to local legend, ancient giants once shaped the land here. Today, hikers follow scenic trails that offer unforgettable views of the falls year-round.

NIAGARA FALLS: LARGEST WATERFALL BY VOLUME IN EASTERN NORTH AMERICA

Every second, more than 3,000 tons of water thunder over Niagara Falls—enough to fill an Olympic-sized swimming pool in just 11 seconds. While not the tallest, Niagara is one of the most powerful waterfalls in the world. It has been steadily eroding backward for over 12,000 years, inching closer to Lake Erie. Millions of visitors ride the Maid of the Mist boats each year to get a closer (and much wetter) view.

LAKE PLACID: HOST OF TWO WINTER OLYMPICS

Lake Placid is one of only three places in the world to host the Winter Olympics twice—first in 1932 and again in 1980. The 1980 Games were the site of the legendary "Miracle on Ice," when the underdog U.S. hockey team beat the heavily favored Soviet Union.

Today, the town embraces its Olympic legacy with murals, memorabilia, and an Olympic museum. Visitors can even ride a real bobsled down the old track—though it's definitely tamer than the Olympic version.

ST. LAWRENCE COUNTY: NEW YORK'S LARGEST COUNTY

Covering 2,821 square miles (7,307 km^2), St. Lawrence County is nearly the size of Delaware and Rhode Island combined. It includes parts of the Adirondack Mountains and the Thousand Islands region.

Despite its vast size, it has a relatively small population—just under 110,000 people—making it an ideal destination for hikers, paddlers, and anyone who loves wide-open spaces.

HISTORIC FARMING TRADITION

New York State is home to some of the oldest continuously operating farms in the United States. For example, Philipsburg Manor, founded in 1693, now operates as a living history museum.

In places like the Hudson Valley and Long Island, many farms have remained in the same families for generations, earning "Century Farm" status for 100 years or more of continuous ownership. Visitors can enjoy apple picking, pumpkin patches, honey tastings, and farmers markets filled with both produce and history.

DID YOU KNOW?

New York holds a world record for the largest gathering of people dressed as fruit. In 2015, over 600 people showed up in Times Square wearing banana, apple, and grape costumes to promote healthy eating.

10

NEW YORK HOLIDAYS & TRADITIONS

New York knows how to throw a party—whether it's a centuries-old cultural festival, a quirky local ritual, or a glittering spectacle broadcast around the globe. From the dazzling lights of the Rockefeller Center Christmas Tree to the zany fun of the No Pants Subway Ride, New Yorkers celebrate in ways that are bold, diverse, and unforgettable.

ICONIC ANNUAL CELEBRATIONS

TRIBUTE IN LIGHT

Every September 11 since 2002, Tribute in Light sends two towering columns of light into the night sky above Lower Manhattan, honoring the Twin Towers. Created using 88 high-powered searchlights, the beams rise up to four miles (6.4 kilom) and can be seen from as far as 60 miles (97 kilom) away.

Because the display coincides with peak fall migration, thousands of individual birds can sometimes become disoriented and circle within the light. Trained volunteers and ornithologists closely monitor the skies and briefly pause the lights when needed, allowing the birds to safely disperse before the tribute resumes.

TIMES SQUARE BALL DROP

This iconic New Year's Eve tradition began in 1907 as a safer replacement for fireworks. The original 700-pound (318 kg) ball was made of iron and wood, and lit by 100 incandescent bulbs.

Crystal-covered Times Square ball. Photo via Clare Cridland, CC BY 2.0, via Wikimedia Commons

Today's crystal-covered sphere weighs nearly 12,000 pounds (5,443 kg) and glows with more than 32,000 LED lights capable of millions of color combinations. About a million people pack Times Square each year to see it drop.

At the same time, a lesser-known tradition—the Wishing Wall —lets visitors write down their hopes for the new year. The wishes are printed on confetti and fall from the sky at midnight.

MACY'S THANKSGIVING DAY PARADE

First held in 1924, the parade originally featured live animals borrowed from the Central Park Zoo. Giant balloons along the route debuted in 1927, starting with Felix the Cat. Today, balloons require up to 90 handlers each and are filled with thousands of cubic feet of helium. During World War II, the parade was paused and the rubber from balloons was donated to the war effort. In 2006, a helium shortage forced Macy's to experiment with air-filled balloons and redesigned tethers.

Local Tip: The balloon inflation the night before the parade, near the American Museum of Natural History, is a lesser-known gem. It's family-friendly and lets visitors see the giant characters up close before they float down the parade route the next morning.

ROCKEFELLER CENTER CHRISTMAS TREE

Rockefeller Center has marked the start of New York's holiday season since 1933. Each year, the festivities officially kick off with the tree-lighting ceremony in late November, typically on the Wednesday after Thanksgiving.

The towering Norway spruce is usually 75 to 100 feet tall (23– 30 m) and is wrapped in more than 50,000 LED lights. It is crowned with a 900-pound (408 kg) Swarovski star containing about 3 million crystals. After the holiday season ends in January, the tree is milled into lumber and donated to Habitat for Humanity, giving the famous tree a second life.

Viewing Tip: For a peaceful experience, visit early—before 7 a.m., or after 10 p.m. when the crowds thin and the lights are still glowing.

***

DID YOU KNOW?

The Rockefeller Center Christmas Tree typically comes from private properties in New York State, New Jersey, or Pennsylvania. Each year, a special selection team searches for a tree that is usually at least 75 feet tall and has a perfect shape.

Once selected, the tree is carefully cut down and transported by truck in a slow-moving convoy to Manhattan. This journey has become a festive event itself, with crowds often gathering along the route to see the enormous tree make its way to Rockefeller Center, officially marking the start of the holiday season in New York City.

***

HOLIDAY WINDOW DISPLAYS

Each December, New York's department stores turn their windows into mini theatrical sets. Saks Fifth Avenue pairs its display with a glittering light show, Bergdorf Goodman leans into artistic couture, and Macy's keeps the nostalgia alive with animated storybook scenes.

Insider Advice: Start at Bloomingdale's and walk down Fifth Avenue past Saks to Macy's Herald Square. Go on a weekday evening before 7 p.m. for the perfect mix of festive buzz and elbow room.

THE RADIO CITY CHRISTMAS SPECTACULAR

The Rockettes have performed this beloved holiday show since 1933, thrilling audiences with high kicks, sparkling costumes, and timeless routines like the "Parade of the Wooden Soldiers" and the Living Nativity.

Best Seats: Orchestra rows F through L give you a centered view of the Rockettes' legendary precision. Morning shows tend to have smaller crowds and more budget-friendly ticket options.

HOLIDAY MARKETS

From mid-November to late December, pop-up markets bring European-style charm to New York's plazas and parks. Bryant Park's Winter Village features over 170 artisan booths and a free-admission ice rink (as long as you bring your own skates). Union Square's market is ideal for handmade gifts, while Columbus Circle offers stunning views of Central Park.

Local Secret: For a cozier experience, head indoors to the Grand Central Holiday Fair. It's warm, festive, and full of gourmet treats that make for a great on-the-go picnic.

THE LILAC FESTIVAL

Each May, Rochester's Highland Park bursts into bloom during North America's largest lilac festival. Over 500 varieties of lilacs paint the gardens in soft purples, pinks, and whites, perfuming the air with their sweet scent.

Best Viewing: Early mornings are the most fragrant, when cool air and morning dew help the scent linger. Visiting on a weekday also means fewer crowds. Don't miss the hidden "Secret Garden," where some of the rarest lilac varieties bloom away from the main paths.

MERMAID PARADE

Mermaid Parade participant. Photo by
Following NYC via pexels.com

This whimsical summer tradition takes place each June at Coney Island. Launched in 1983, the Mermaid Parade is part performance art, part costume contest, and all New York.

Thousands of participants dress as mermaids, mermen, sea creatures, pirates, and more.

Past parade royalty has included celebrities like Lou Reed and Queen Latifah. The event draws over 800,000 spectators and celebrates creativity, self-expression, and Coney Island's quirky carnival spirit. Anyone can join—costume encouraged!

CULTURAL & COMMUNITY TRADITIONS

HAUDENOSAUNEE GREEN CORN CEREMONY

Each summer, the Haudenosaunee (Iroquois) nations of upstate New York give thanks for the corn harvest with a multi-day celebration filled with traditional dances, songs, and communal feasting.

This centuries-old thanksgiving ceremony is a time of renewal and gratitude. Some communities welcome respectful visitors to observe and learn from these living Indigenous traditions.

THREE KINGS DAY PARADE

Since 1977, East Harlem has hosted a joyful parade every January 6th to mark Día de los Reyes, or Three Kings Day—a cherished holiday in many Latin American cultures.

The event features giant puppets, lively music, colorful costumes, and even live camels, highlighting the area's rich Puerto Rican, Dominican, and broader Latino heritage.

SYRACUSE WINTERFEST

For more than 35 years, Syracuse has leaned into its snowy reputation with Winterfest—a quirky cold-weather celebration featuring ice carving contests, cook-offs, and offbeat events like the "Stupid Hat Contest" and "Human Dogsled Race." With over 100,000 visitors annually, it's a frosty love letter to upstate winter fun.

PINKSTER FESTIVAL

What began as a Dutch Pentecost tradition in the 1600s became a powerful celebration of African American community and culture during colonial times. Enslaved and free Black New Yorkers transformed Pinkster into a festival of music, dance, and connection. Today, historic sites revive the tradition with African drumming, storytelling, and performances each May.

PICKLE DAY (LOWER EAST SIDE)

Once the heart of New York's pickle trade, the Lower East Side now celebrates its tangy roots each October. Pickle Day is a crunchy, quirky street fair where visitors can sample everything from classic kosher dills to spicy kimchi, alongside games, food vendors, and nods to the area's rich Jewish, Chinese, and Puerto Rican history.

LUNAR NEW YEAR CELEBRATIONS

New York's Chinatowns—especially in Manhattan, Queens, and Brooklyn—burst to life each winter with Lunar New Year parades, lion dances, firecrackers, and traditional performances. These celebrations honor the start of the new year in Chinese, Korean, Vietnamese, and other East and Southeast Asian cultures, welcoming good luck and community joy.

UNIQUE & QUIRKY TRADITIONS

FIRE HYDRANT SPRAY CAPS

On hot summer days, fire hydrants in New York City are often topped with special spray caps that transform them into makeshift fountains. It's a tradition that turns city streets into splash zones—especially in neighborhoods without easy access to pools—creating spontaneous fun for kids and adults alike.

SUMMER STREET FESTIVALS

When warm weather arrives, many New York City streets temporarily close to traffic for neighborhood festivals. Blocks transform into lively pedestrian zones filled with food vendors, music, craft stalls, and community activities. From Manhattan's Columbus Avenue to Brooklyn's neighborhood fairs, these summer street festivals turn ordinary streets into spontaneous celebrations of local culture.

New York City also hosts **Summer Streets**, a special program each August when nearly 7 miles (11 km) of Manhattan streets close to cars for a day so people can walk, bike, dance, and enjoy free activities across the city.

GREENMARKETS IN THE CITY

Farmers markets pop up across New York City throughout the week, bringing fresh produce from regional farms into urban neighborhoods. One of the most popular takes place near the American Museum of Natural History on Manhattan's Upper West Side, where locals gather to shop for seasonal fruits, baked goods, and handmade foods.

BLESSING OF THE ANIMALS

Every October, the Cathedral of St. John the Divine opens its massive doors to creatures great and small—from dogs and cats to llamas, camels, and peacocks. Inspired by St. Francis of Assisi, this charming ceremony draws crowds who come to have their pets blessed in one of the world's largest Gothic cathedrals.

DOUBLE DUTCH JUMP ROPE COMPETITIONS

Double Dutch has deep roots in New York's African American communities and has evolved into a high-energy sport. Each spring, competitions across schools and recreation centers lead up to show-stopping finals held in historic venues like the Apollo Theater in Harlem, a neighborhood in Upper Manhattan, where teams wow audiences with athleticism, rhythm, and creativity.

NO PANTS SUBWAY RIDE

What started as a prank in 2002 by a comedy group has become a global tradition. Every January, hundreds of participants board NYC subway trains in full winter gear—minus their pants. The goal? Act completely normal and confuse commuters. It's a chilly, hilarious celebration of urban absurdity.

STATEN ISLAND CHUCK (GROUNDHOG DAY)

Move over, Groundhog forecaster Punxsutawney Phil—New York has its own weather-predicting groundhog. A groundhog (also called a woodchuck) is a large burrowing rodent that hibernates during winter.

Every year on Groundhog Day (February 2), tradition says that if the groundhog emerges from its burrow and sees its shadow, winter will last six more weeks. If it doesn't see its shadow, spring will arrive early.

Staten Island Chuck has been making this "prediction" since 1981 and famously bit Mayor Michael Bloomberg during the ceremony in 2009. Local legend claims Chuck is more accurate than his Pennsylvania counterpart, and crowds gather each year to see what he predicts.

FEAST OF SAN GENNARO

For over 90 years, the streets of Little Italy have erupted in color, music, and mouth-watering aromas each September during the Feast of San Gennaro. What began as a religious celebration is now a massive street fair complete with cannoli-eating contests, live music, and parades honoring the patron saint of Naples.

DYKER HEIGHTS CHRISTMAS LIGHTS

In Brooklyn's Dyker Heights, "go big or go home" is the motto each December. What began as a friendly neighborhood competition now attracts professional decorators, bus tours, and visitors from around the world. Expect dazzling displays of lights, mechanical elves, rooftop reindeer, and front yards that rival theme parks.

HISTORICAL & COMMEMORATIVE EVENTS

EVACUATION DAY

Once a major New York City holiday, Evacuation Day marked

the 1783 withdrawal of British troops at the end of the Revolutionary War. Celebrated each November 25 with parades and fireworks well into the 19th century, it symbolized hard-won independence and New York's pivotal place in that history.

Though no longer widely observed, a flag-raising tradition still takes place each year at Bowling Green in Lower Manhattan.

BATTLE OF BROOKLYN COMMEMORATION

Every August, Brooklyn honors the largest battle of the Revolutionary War with reenactments, memorial services, and history-themed events. Activities often take place at Green-Wood Cemetery and Prospect Park, both of which sit on former battlefields. The commemoration shines a light on sacrifices made by those fighting for freedom, and New York's central place in that effort.

JUNETEENTH

Now an official state holiday, Juneteenth celebrates the end of slavery in the United States. Across New York, especially in Harlem and Bedford-Stuyvesant, communities come together with parades, concerts, educational programming, and joyful gatherings that honor freedom and resilience.

NYC PRIDE PARADE

Each June, millions gather in Manhattan for the NYC Pride Parade, one of the largest LGBTQ+ celebrations in the world. The parade commemorates the 1969 Stonewall Riots in Greenwich Village, widely considered a turning point in the modern LGBTQ+ rights movement. Today, the event features colorful floats, marching groups, music, and celebrations of equality and inclusion along Fifth Avenue and through Greenwich Village.

PUERTO RICAN DAY PARADE

Held every June along Manhattan's Fifth Avenue, the Puerto Rican Day Parade is one of the largest cultural parades in the country. Colorful floats, traditional music and dance, and millions of attendees celebrate Puerto Rican pride and the community's rich contributions to American life.

EASTER PARADE AND BONNET FESTIVAL

Since the 1870s, New Yorkers have taken to Fifth Avenue on Easter Sunday wearing imaginative and often outrageous hats. There are no floats or marching bands, just people showing off bonnets decorated with live birds, miniature Ferris wheels, and all sorts of whimsical creations. The tradition even inspired the classic musical Easter Parade.

POLAR BEAR PLUNGE

On New Year's Day, brave swimmers gather at Coney Island to leap into the icy Atlantic Ocean. This frosty tradition, dating back to 1903, is run by the Coney Island Polar Bear Club and also raises money for local charities. It's one of the chilliest and quirkiest ways New Yorkers ring in the new year.

SARATOGA RACING SEASON

Since 1863, the Saratoga Springs racetrack has hosted one of the most celebrated horse racing seasons in the world. Known for its elegance, flower-adorned winners, and lively social scene, the 40-day summer meet draws fans from around the globe.

DROPPING OF THE CARNATIONS

At the Belmont Stakes, the final race in the Triple Crown of major horse races, the winning horse receives a traditional blanket of white carnations. This floral moment dates back to the 1930s and complements the roses of the Kentucky Derby and the black-eyed Susans of the Preakness Stakes.

UNIQUELY NEW YORK

FIRST NIGHT OF SUMMER

As soon as the first truly warm evening arrives, New Yorkers flood parks, rooftops, sidewalks, and patios to celebrate the unofficial end of winter. There's no set date or schedule—just an instant, citywide mood shift. Ice cream lines grow, lawn chairs appear in unlikely places, and the city pulses with shared relief and the anticipation of summer.

TOAST TO THE GHOST OF BABE RUTH

At NYY Steak, a Yankees-themed steakhouse once located near Yankee Stadium, a bell rang each night at exactly 7:14 p.m. Guests would pause to raise a glass and toast Babe Ruth, honoring the baseball slugger's 714 career home runs—one of the most famous records in the history of the sport.

Although the restaurant closed in 2020, the tradition reflected the deep connection New Yorkers feel to their baseball history and to one of the New York Yankees' greatest legends.

EMPIRE STATE BUILDING LIGHTING

The Empire State Building often features different color schemes of lighting at night, to mark everything from national holidays to sports wins to cultural celebrations. The calendar is planned months ahead, but the colors can be updated in less than a minute in response to breaking news or special moments. It's one of the most visible ways New York expresses itself.

SANTACON

Every December, thousands of people dressed as Santas, elves, and snowmen descend on NYC for a citywide bar crawl known as SantaCon. What started as a small performance art protest in San Francisco now lives on in New York as a chaotic mix of holiday cheer, costume creativity, and rowdy revelry.

DID YOU KNOW?

Ticker-tape parade for astronaut, Gordon Cooper, celebrating the final flight of the Mercury program in 1963. Photo via NASA, Public domain, via Wikimedia Commons

New Yorkers throw more ticker-tape parades than any other city in the world. Ticker tape was the long, narrow paper used by early stock ticker machines to print stock prices. In the late 1800s, office workers would toss the discarded strips out their windows during celebrations, creating a blizzard of paper in the streets below.

The tradition began in 1886, when crowds celebrated the dedication of the Statue of Liberty. Since then, the Canyon of Heroes along Broadway has honored astronauts, world leaders, and championship sports teams—with more than 200 parades and counting.

11

NEW YORK CULTURE AND HOSPITALITY

In New York—especially in New York City—time seems to move faster than almost anywhere else. A "New York minute" is the blink between a traffic light turning green and the car behind you honking.

This quick pace shapes everyday life. Coffee orders are called out rapidly, subway riders weave through crowds with purpose, and conversations often jump straight to the point. For newcomers it can feel intense, but to locals it's simply how the city keeps moving.

URBAN HOSPITALITY & CITY LIFE

DIRECT COMMUNICATION

New Yorkers are famously direct. What might sound blunt to outsiders is usually meant to be helpful. In a city where millions of people share the same sidewalks and subways, clear and straightforward communication saves time for everyone.

If a New Yorker says a restaurant is good, they mean it. And if they give directions, they'll likely get straight to the point—no small talk required.

BODEGA CULTURE

The neighborhood bodega is much more than a corner store. It's a community fixture where the owner might know your go-to sandwich, and the store cat greets customers like a furry concierge. Many bodegas offer credit to regulars, accept packages, and serve as unofficial information desks for the whole block.

DID YOU KNOW?

Many NYC bodegas are home to "bodega cats" who have become local celebrities, controlling rodents and racking up thousands of social media followers.

STOOP CULTURE

In New York, brownstone stoops are the city's answer to front porches. Neighbors gather on these steps to chat, sip iced coffee, or catch a summer breeze. From yard sales to sidewalk concerts, stoops create a sense of street-level connection in a city known for towering skyscrapers.

THE SUBWAY NOD

Regular subway riders often exchange a simple nod with familiar faces. It's a quiet sign of recognition that says, "I see you," without breaking the unspoken rule of subway privacy. This tiny gesture captures New York's unique blend of independence and community.

HELPING LOST TOURISTS

Despite their tough reputation, New Yorkers are surprisingly helpful to visitors. If someone looks lost with a map, chances are a local will step in. Some will even walk blocks out of their way to help. Whether through hand gestures, phone apps, or paper napkin maps, they'll get you where you need to go.

FIRE ESCAPE GATHERINGS

Party on the fire escape. Photo by Following NYC via pexels.com

Fire escapes become vertical balconies in summer where friends share meals, conversations, and stargaze. These metal perches exemplify New Yorkers' knack for creating connection even in tight urban spaces.

During the COVID-19 pandemic in 2020, many New Yorkers also stepped onto their fire escapes or leaned out their windows each evening to cheer for doctors, nurses, and essential workers.

THE ART OF LINE WAITING

Waiting in line is its own cultural event. People hold spots for friends, chat with strangers, share insider tips, and even bring folding chairs for overnight waits at popular venues like free theater ticket lines.

DINER HOSPITALITY

Classic diners serve everyone from Wall Street execs to construction workers with warm familiarity. Regulars have "their table," where servers know their coffee and order by heart.

DID YOU KNOW?

Some NYC diners have regular tables informally reserved for customers who visit at the same day and time weekly, maintained by institutional memory.

"YOU GOOD?"

This phrase captures New York hospitality's mix of efficiency and care. It's both a quick check-in by servers and a supportive text from friends, offering help without demanding explanation.

HOLDING THE DOOR

A small courtesy that binds New Yorkers, the door-holding chain often stretches through a dozen people, punctuated by quick nods or "thank-yous," creating a web of daily kindness.

COMMUNITY GARDENS

Volunteer-run gardens transform vacant lots into vibrant green spaces for neighbors to gather, celebrate harvests, and host cultural events. A "garden key" system ensures shared stewardship.

WEATHER SOLIDARITY

From digging out buried cars after snowstorms to helping a neighbor carry groceries during a heatwave, New Yorkers show up when extreme weather hits. Lending umbrellas, sharing generators, or checking on neighbors—New York's resilience often shines brightest in a storm.

UPSTATE & RURAL TRADITIONS

UPSTATE BARN RAISING

In farming towns throughout the Finger Lakes and Hudson Valley, barn raisings are still a living tradition. Neighbors gather to build or repair a barn in a single day, ending with a communal meal to celebrate the effort and connection.

FINGER LAKES WINE TOURS

Unlike many large commercial wine regions, Finger Lakes wineries are often small and family-run. Visitors might find the winemaker personally pouring the tastings and chatting about the vineyard. Some guests sign the visitor book, and loyal regulars occasionally lend a hand during harvest or bottling.

ADIRONDACK HOSPITALITY

The Adirondacks are known for "wilderness hospitality," with public shelters for hikers, trail registers with supplies, and locals sharing advice about hidden swimming holes and safe hiking routes.

HUDSON VALLEY HARVEST SWAPS

Home gardeners and foragers in the Hudson Valley often host informal harvest swaps where no money changes hands. Instead, people trade jars of jam, baskets of zucchini, and hand-written recipes—along with the latest neighborhood updates.

NORTH COUNTRY WINTER ADAPTATIONS

Near the Canadian border, unheated porches double as winter refrigerators. Neighbors share snowblowers, lend generators during power outages, and make a habit of checking on one another when storms roll through.

TOMPKINS COUNTY DISH-TO-PASS

In the Finger Lakes, potlucks known as "dish-to-pass" gatherings feature locally sourced dishes and detailed ingredient lists to accommodate dietary needs. These shared meals are woven into community life, appearing at celebrations, fundraisers, and even some local meetings.

REGIONAL & CIVIC HOSPITALITY

BUFFALO'S "CITY OF GOOD NEIGHBORS" ETHOS

Buffalo's community spirit shines brightest during moments of crisis. During blizzards like "Snowvember," residents form human chains to rescue stranded motorists and open their homes to complete strangers. On regular days, that same generosity is seen in tailgate parties that welcome opposing fans and extra seats always offered at the table.

DID YOU KNOW?

During the 2022 Christmas blizzard, a man broke into a school to shelter 24 stranded people and pets, then cleaned up and left a note. The city rewarded him with Buffalo Bills football playoff tickets.

ALBANY'S CAPITAL ACCESSIBILITY

Albany's small downtown and walkable neighborhoods make government feel approachable. It's not unusual to run into lawmakers or state workers at local cafés and pubs, blurring the line between political life and community connection.

THOUSAND ISLANDS BOAT HOSPITALITY

In the Thousand Islands, hospitality floats on water. Boaters invite others to tie up for shared meals, fishing tips, or sunset cocktails. Many private docks are open to those in need of supplies or shelter, turning the waterways into a welcoming neighborhood.

TUG HILL REGION'S WINTER FRIENDLINESS

The Tug Hill Plateau, known for some of the heaviest snowfall in the eastern U.S., has a strong tradition of neighborly support during brutal winters. Residents share snowplows, organize community snow removal efforts, and routinely check on each other to keep isolated rural areas safe and connected.

ITHACA'S COLLEGE TOWN WARMTH

Ithaca, home to Cornell University and Ithaca College, blends academic culture with small-town friendliness. Local businesses often host "welcome weeks" for new students, featuring free community dinners, concerts, and volunteer opportunities that integrate newcomers into the fabric of the town.

SARATOGA SPRINGS HOSPITALITY

Known for its horse racing season, Saratoga Springs embraces visitors with a longstanding tradition of elegant social events, garden parties, and open-air concerts. The town's small size and walkability make it easy for tourists to mingle with locals, creating an inviting atmosphere.

CAPITAL REGION'S FARMERS MARKETS

Upstate New York's Capital Region hosts vibrant farmers markets where growers personally engage with shoppers, sharing stories about their crops and recipes. These markets often double as social hubs, where neighbors connect and strengthen community bonds.

HUDSON VALLEY ARTIST COMMUNITIES

The Hudson Valley's artist enclaves, like Woodstock and Beacon, have a tradition of open studios and community art fairs, where artists welcome visitors into their homes and workshops. These events foster cultural exchange and create informal hospitality networks centered around creativity.

DID YOU KNOW?

New Yorkers help fight food insecurity through community fridges, also known as freedges. These public refrigerators, found everywhere from Brooklyn sidewalks to upstate church lots, are stocked and maintained by volunteers.

The Peoples Peoples Community Fridge in Manhattan. Photo via Jim.henderson, CC BY 4.0, via Wikimedia Commons

Anyone can take what they need or leave what they can—no questions asked. With locations in both big cities and rural towns, freedges are a grassroots example of everyday hospitality across the state.

12

INDUSTRY AND
ECONOMY OF NEW YORK

New York isn't just a cultural icon—it's an economic giant. From Wall Street traders to Adirondack dairy farmers, the Empire State is fueled by a remarkable mix of industries. Whether you're watching a Broadway show, sipping a Finger Lakes wine, or sending a package through the Port of New York, you're part of one of the most powerful economies in the world.

FINANCIAL SERVICES

Known as the financial capital of the world, New York City's Wall Street is the beating heart of global finance. The New York Stock Exchange, founded in 1792, is the world's largest stock exchange by market capitalization, with listed companies worth over $25 trillion. The financial services industry employs more than 330,000 people in New York State and contributes approximately 20-25% of the city's economic output.

Beyond Wall Street, New York hosts major banks, insurance companies, hedge funds, and private equity firms that fund startups and support real estate development.

The bronze Charging Bull near Wall Street is a symbol of financial resilience and optimism. It was originally placed as an act of guerrilla art and removed by city officials. After public outcry, it was returned and is now one of the most-photographed statues in New York.

MEDIA AND ENTERTAINMENT

New York is a global hub for media and entertainment. Major networks like NBC, ABC, CBS, and Fox are based here, along with streaming platforms like HBO and Netflix. The state hosts more than 250 television shows and 200 movies each year, generating an estimated 60-70 billion dollars in economic activity.

Publishing is also big business. All of the Big Five book publishers are headquartered in Manhattan, supporting a publishing industry that fuels over 320,000 media jobs.

SNL ECONOMIC IMPACT

Saturday Night Live, filmed at NBC's Rockefeller Center since 1975, has helped define American comedy for generations, and continues to boost New York's economy through tourism and media production.

TECHNOLOGY

Silicon Alley in NYC evolved from a small startup cluster in the 1990s to a tech giant rivaling Silicon Valley, with over 9,000 startups and offices for Google, Facebook, and Amazon.

The Brooklyn Navy Yard is now a tech manufacturing hub, while Rochester and Buffalo specialize in optics, photonics, biotech, and medical devices. The tech sector employs over 300,000 people statewide, contributing about $125 billion annually.

DID YOU KNOW?

Etsy started as a small Brooklyn startup and helped kick off the borough's creative economy boom!

FASHION AND RETAIL

Once producing 95% of the clothing sold in the United States, New York City remains America's fashion capital, hosting New York Fashion Week, which generates about $900 million and draws 150,000 visitors.

Macy's Herald Square once held the title of the world's largest department store. Today, the fashion industry employs more than 180,000 New Yorkers. While the industry faces growing scrutiny over environmental and labor practices, a rising number of designers and organizations in the city are working to promote more sustainable and ethical fashion.

HEALTHCARE

New York has over 250 hospitals, including world-renowned centers like Memorial Sloan Kettering Cancer Center and Mount Sinai Health System. Healthcare is the state's largest employer, with 1.2 million workers and $175 billion in economic activity.

The state attracts about $2.3 billion annually from the National Institutes of Health (NIH)—the U.S. government's primary medical research funding agency—powering medical breakthroughs and supporting a growing biotech sector with more than 350 companies.

DID YOU KNOW?

The first successful heart transplant in the U.S. was performed at Columbia University Medical Center here in NYC!

TOURISM

Before the COVID-19 pandemic in 2020, New York City attracted about 66.6 million tourists each year, who spent more than $46 billion annually during their visits. Iconic landmarks like the Statue of Liberty and Central Park draw millions of visitors, alongside natural treasures across the state such as Adirondack Park and the Finger Lakes wine region.

Tourism supports over 825,000 jobs statewide. Broadway theaters alone generate about $14.7 billion in economic impact and support nearly 97,000 jobs. The city also boasts around 150 Michelin-recognized restaurants, making it one of the world's top culinary destinations.

TOURISM TAX

Tourists contribute $8.7 billion in state and local taxes yearly, offsetting costs for New Yorkers and funding public services.

AGRICULTURE

New York ranks in the top five U.S. states for apples, maple syrup, dairy, and cabbage production. The dairy industry alone includes about 4,000 farms, producing roughly 15 billion pounds of milk each year—about 1.7 billion gallons (6.6 billion liters).

New York is also the third-largest wine producer in the United States, with more than 450 wineries, many located in the

Finger Lakes. Major crops such as apples, cabbage, sweet corn, and pumpkins support over 55,000 agricultural jobs statewide.

MANUFACTURING

Manufacturing in New York focuses on high-value industries like aerospace (Lockheed Martin), specialty foods, semiconductors, optics, and medical devices. This sector employs 430,000 people and contributes $75 billion to the economy.

REAL ESTATE

New York's real estate market is one of the world's most valuable and dynamic, with Manhattan prices averaging over $1,500 per square foot. The Hudson Yards project is the largest private real estate development in U.S. history at $25 billion. The real estate sector employs over 300,000 people and generates $15 billion annually in state and local taxes.

EDUCATION

New York is home to more than 300 colleges and universities, including world-renowned institutions like Columbia, Cornell, and NYU.

Higher education is a major economic engine in the state, employing around 180,000 people and contributing an estimated $88 billion annually to the economy.

The State University of New York (SUNY) and City University of New York (CUNY) systems not only educate hundreds of thousands of students but also support local economies across the state. Campuses generate jobs, attract research funding, and boost spending in housing, food, and transportation.

DID YOU KNOW?

International students at New York's universities contribute over $5 billion annually to the state economy, fueling innovation and local businesses.

ARTS AND CULTURE

New York has more than 2,000 arts organizations, making culture a major part of the state's identity and economy.

Across upstate New York, regional institutions in cities like Buffalo, Rochester, and Albany anchor tourism, support local artists, and help revitalize downtown neighborhoods.

In New York City, some of the world's most famous cultural institutions draw millions of visitors each year. The Metropolitan Museum of Art welcomes more than 7 million visitors annually and generates about $1 billion in economic impact. The Lincoln Center for the Performing Arts contributes roughly $3.4 billion each year through performances, education programs, and tourism.

Altogether, New York's arts sector supports roughly 300,000 to 350,000 jobs statewide.

PORT OF NEW YORK AND NEW JERSEY

The Port of New York and New Jersey is the third-largest port in the United States, handling more than 7.5 million shipping containers valued at roughly $200 billion each year. The port supports about 400,000 jobs and generates $8.5 billion in annual tax revenue.

To accommodate larger modern cargo ships, major infrastructure upgrades were required. One of the most dramatic was the raising of the Bayonne Bridge, where engineers lifted the roadway by 64 feet (19.5 m)—the largest bridge-raising project of its kind.

This permanent change allowed massive container ships to pass beneath the bridge, helping cargo volume at the port grow by about 30% over the past decade.

RENEWABLE ENERGY

New York is a national leader in clean-energy policy and growth, with some of the most ambitious targets in the country. The state aims to generate 70% of its electricity from renewable sources by 2030 and reach carbon neutrality by 2050.

Massive offshore wind projects are expected to create more than 10,000 jobs, while solar power capacity has grown by over 2,100% since 2011. Today, clean energy employs roughly 150,000 workers statewide, making it a major and rapidly expanding part of New York's economy.

CRAFT BEVERAGE INDUSTRY

Brewing has deep roots in New York. One of the earliest breweries in what is now New York City opened in 1612 on Brewers Street in New Amsterdam, reflecting the Dutch settlers' strong brewing traditions.

Today, New York's craft beverage industry is booming. The state has more than 400 craft breweries, 200 wineries, 180 distilleries, and 65 cider producers. The industry has grown over 500% in the past decade, generating about $5 billion annually and supporting rural economies.

New York also created a unique Farm Brewery license, which rewards brewers who use ingredients grown in the state. In exchange for sourcing New York hops, barley, fruit, or honey, breweries receive special privileges such as operating tasting rooms, selling beer by the glass, and distributing their own products. The program helps support both craft brewers and New York farmers.

MINIMUM WAGE AND TAXES

As of 2025, minimum wage is $16 in NYC, Long Island, and Westchester; $15 elsewhere. New York's minimum wage is among the highest in the U.S., reflecting the high cost of living and progressive labor policies.

New York's progressive income tax ranges from 4% to 10.9%, with the highest rate on incomes over $25 million, funding essential public services.

DID YOU KNOW?

New York State is the nation's third-largest producer of grapes —and nearly all of them are grown outside of NYC. These grapes are mostly grown in the Finger Lakes, Lake Erie, and Hudson Valley regions. The grapes fuel not only the state's 450+ wineries, but also juice, jelly, and grape pie industries. In fact, the town of Naples, NY, holds an annual Grape Festival celebrating its locally famous Concord grape pie!

13

HIGHER EDUCATION IN NEW YORK

New York isn't just a cultural and financial powerhouse—it's also an education giant. With historic institutions, trailblazing campuses, and some of the largest public university systems in the country, the Empire State has helped shape higher learning for more than two centuries.

PUBLIC UNIVERSITIES (SUNY & CUNY)

THE NATION'S LARGEST PUBLIC SYSTEM
The State University of New York—better known as SUNY—is the largest public university system in the United States. With 64 campuses and more than 400,000 enrolled students, it covers everything from community colleges to elite research institutions like SUNY Stony Brook and SUNY Albany.

BORN FROM THE GI BILL
SUNY was officially established in 1948, in part to serve World War II veterans returning under the Servicemen's Readjustment Act of 1944, better known as the GI Bill—a U.S. law passed by Congress that provided returning soldiers with benefits such as funding for college education.

Its creation helped open the doors of higher education to a much broader and more diverse student population across New York State.

CUNY'S RADICAL ROOTS

The City University of New York (CUNY) began as the Free
Academy in 1847—founded to provide a tuition-free education to the children of immigrants and working-class families.
Today, it includes 25 colleges and serves more than 225,000
degree-seeking students across New York City's five
boroughs.

OPENING DOORS TO THE WORLD

CUNY is one of the most diverse university systems in the
country. More than 40% of its students were born outside the
U.S., and over 150 different languages are spoken across its
campuses—from Haitian Creole to Urdu.

ALBANY'S NUCLEAR REACTOR

SUNY Albany is one of the only public universities in the U.S.
with a licensed nuclear research reactor on campus. It's used
strictly for research and education—not power generation—and
helps train future nuclear scientists and engineers.

IVY LEAGUE & ELITE
PRIVATE SCHOOLS

COLUMBIA: NEW YORK'S OLDEST UNIVERSITY

Founded in 1754 as King's College, Columbia University is the
oldest institution of higher learning in New York. Located in
Manhattan's Morningside Heights, it has produced U.S. presi-
dents, Nobel laureates, and iconic creatives—including the
founders of both the Pulitzer Prizes and the Modern Language
Association.

IVY LEAGUE WITH A VIEW

Cornell University, perched on the edge of Cayuga Lake in Ithaca, is one of the only Ivy League schools located outside a major city. Its hilltop campus is known for stunning gorges and waterfalls, giving students a front-row seat to some of Upstate New York's most dramatic natural beauty.

A SCHOOL FOR "ANY PERSON, ANY STUDY"

Cornell's founding motto—"I would found an institution where any person can find instruction in any study"—was groundbreaking in 1865. From the beginning, Cornell admitted women and students of all races, religions, and social classes, a rarity among elite schools of the time.

COLUMBIA AND THE ATOMIC AGE

Columbia played a key role in launching the atomic age. Physicists at the university—including Nobel Prize–winner Enrico Fermi—helped lay the groundwork for the Manhattan Project, the top-secret effort that developed the first nuclear weapons during World War II.

DID YOU KNOW?

New York has one of the highest concentrations of Nobel Prize winners in the world. Many have studied or worked at institutions like Columbia University, NYU, and Cornell. These academic centers have helped fuel groundbreaking discoveries and innovations that connect education, science, and the economy.

BARNARD: A WOMEN'S COLLEGE WITH IVY STATUS

Barnard College, founded in 1889, is an elite women's liberal arts college affiliated with Columbia University. Barnard students take many classes at Columbia, but graduate with their own degree—making it one of the few remaining women's colleges with Ivy League access.

HOW THE IVY LEAGUE GOT ITS NAME

The term Ivy League didn't originally mean elite academics—it started as the name of a college sports conference formed in 1954. But the nickname was applied to schools in part because of , the ivy-covered buildings common on those historic campuses. And the name stuck. Of the eight Ivy League schools, two are in New York State: Columbia University in Manhattan and Cornell University in Ithaca.

GROUNDBREAKING SCHOOLS

VASSAR COLLEGE OPENED DOORS FOR WOMEN

Vassar College was founded in 1861 in Poughkeepsie as one of the first higher education institutions for women in the United States. It offered rigorous academics equal to men's colleges at the time. The school became coeducational in 1969 but remains known for its trailblazing role in women's education.

THE COOPER UNION OFFERED FREE EDUCATION FROM DAY ONE

When inventor Peter Cooper established The Cooper Union

in 1859, he made it tuition-free and open to all, regardless of race, gender, or income. For over 150 years, every student attended for free. Although full scholarships are no longer guaranteed, the school still offers one of the most generous aid programs in the country.

BARD COLLEGE BRINGS COLLEGE INTO PRISONS

The Bard Prison Initiative allows incarcerated people to earn accredited college degrees through Bard College. Students in the program take rigorous courses taught by Bard professors. In 2015, Bard's debate team famously defeated Harvard in a public debate, drawing national attention.

NEW YORK PIONEERED DEAF EDUCATION

The New York School for the Deaf was founded in 1817 in Manhattan and was one of the first schools in the country for deaf students. It played a key role in the early development of American Sign Language. The school still exists today and is now located in White Plains.

EARLY COMPUTER SCIENCE FOR WOMEN

In the 1960s, Marymount Manhattan College offered one of the first computer science degree programs in the country specifically for women. This helped open the tech world to female students at a time when the field was almost entirely male.

NY CAMPUS CURIOSITIES

A CULINARY SCHOOL WITH A NO-CHOCOLATE RULE

At the Culinary Institute of America in Hyde Park, pastry students aren't allowed to work with chocolate until they've mastered the basics—including precise measurements, classic doughs, sugar work, and temperature control. The rule forces students to develop accuracy and discipline before tackling chocolate, one of pastry's most finicky ingredients.

The CIA (no relation to the spy agency) is widely regarded as one of the top culinary schools in the world, known for its rigorous, technique-first approach.

A COLLEGE BUILT INTO A SKYSCRAPER

Baruch College in Manhattan operates out of the 17-story Newman Vertical Campus, one of the tallest college buildings in the country. With elevators instead of quads and sweeping city views from its classrooms, it's a very different kind of campus experience.

ALFRED UNIVERSITY HAS A GLASS-BLOWING PROGRAM

Alfred University, located in western New York, is known for its College of Ceramics and world-class glass engineering labs. Students there don't just study—it's one of the only places in the country where you can earn credit for blowing glass and designing kilns.

A LAUNDRY CHUTE FOR BOOKS

The library at SUNY Geneseo has a system of book delivery

chutes that look like laundry drop-offs in an old mansion. It was designed so students could order books from upper floors and have them dropped down to the checkout desk—no hiking through the stacks required.

DID YOU KNOW?

More than 1.2 million students attend colleges and universities across New York State. That's more people than live in the entire state of Montana. From ivy-covered lecture halls in Manhattan to glass-blowing studios in western New York, the Empire State might just be the most diverse classroom in the country.

14

NEW YORK STATE SPORTS

From backyard stickball to Olympic gold, New York knows how to play. Whether it's a sold-out night at Yankee Stadium, a double Dutch competition in Brooklyn, or a serene morning of fly fishing in the Catskills, the Empire State is bursting with athletic energy. It's the only state where you can snowboard, play streetball, skate, and scream at a Subway Series baseball game—all in one weekend (if you're ambitious).

NO OFFICIAL STATE SPORT

New York doesn't have an official state sport, but that doesn't stop the Empire State from being one of the world's premier sporting destinations. From iconic teams in New York City to outdoor adventures in the Adirondacks, sports are deeply woven into the fabric of New York culture.

PROFESSIONAL SPORTS LANDSCAPE

New York is one of the most sports-rich states in the country, with eleven teams across five major leagues and some of the most famous franchises in the world.

The New York metropolitan area is the only region in the United States with two MLB teams, two NBA teams, two NHL teams, and two MLS teams—creating some of the country's most intense sports rivalries.

MAJOR LEAGUE BASEBALL (MLB)

NEW YORK YANKEES

The Yankees, founded in 1901, are baseball's most successful franchise. Playing at Yankee Stadium in the Bronx, the team is famous for its 27 World Series championships, its legendary players like Babe Ruth and Derek Jeter, its pinstriped uniforms, and the iconic interlocking "NY" logo.

NEW YORK METS

Founded in 1962, the New York Mets play at Citi Field in Queens and have won two World Series championships (1969 and 1986).

The Mets' distinctive orange and blue colors honor New York's baseball history. The blue comes from the former Brooklyn Dodgers, and the orange from the old New York Giants—two National League teams that left the city in the 1950s. When the Mets were created, the colors symbolized the return of National League baseball to New York.

SUBWAY SERIES

The rivalry games between the Yankees and Mets are called the Subway Series because fans can easily take the subway between stadiums. Between 1921 and 1956, New York teams faced each other in the World Series 13 times!

NATIONAL FOOTBALL LEAGUE (NFL)

BUFFALO BILLS

Founded in 1960, the Buffalo Bills play at Highmark Stadium and famously appeared in four consecutive Super Bowls (1990-1993), losing each time. Bills Mafia, the team's passionate fanbase, is known for energetic tailgating traditions like table-smashing and remarkable charity drives.

NEW YORK GIANTS

Founded in 1925, the New York Giants are one of the NFL's oldest franchises and have won four Super Bowl championships. Although they play their home games at MetLife Stadium in New Jersey, the team's identity remains firmly rooted in New York, where it was founded and built its legacy.

NEW YORK JETS

Founded in 1959 as the New York Titans (the team was renamed the Jets in 1963), the New York Jets represent a different chapter of New York football history.

The team became famous for Joe Namath's bold promise before Super Bowl III in 1969, when he guaranteed the Jets would win against a heavily favored opponent. When the Jets pulled off the upset victory, it shocked fans and helped prove that the newer American Football League could compete with the older National Football League, reshaping the future of professional football.

NATIONAL BASKETBALL ASSOCIATION (NBA)

NEW YORK KNICKS

Established in 1946, the Knicks play at Madison Square Garden, boasting championships in 1970 and 1973. Despite decades without championships, the team enjoys a dedicated fanbase and a lively game atmosphere enhanced by celebrity fans.

BROOKLYN NETS

The Brooklyn Nets relocated from New Jersey to the Barclays Center in 2012, bringing NBA basketball back to Brooklyn for the first time since the Dodgers left the borough in 1957.

The franchise has had a surprisingly nomadic history. It began in 1967 as the New Jersey Americans in the American Basketball Association (ABA), then became the New York Nets, playing at Nassau Veterans Memorial Coliseum on Long Island. After later moving back to New Jersey, the team finally settled in Brooklyn.

Today, the Nets embrace their borough identity with bold "BKLYN" jerseys and a vibrant fan section known as "The Block," creating an energetic Brooklyn atmosphere on game nights.

NATIONAL HOCKEY LEAGUE (NHL)

NEW YORK RANGERS

One of the NHL's original teams (1926), the Rangers, have won four Stanley Cups. They're recognized for their diagonal "RANGERS" jersey text and passionate fans, who chant "Let's Go Rangers!" throughout Madison Square Garden.

NEW YORK ISLANDERS

Founded in 1972, the New York Islanders dominated hockey in the early 1980s, winning four consecutive Stanley Cup championships. Now playing at UBS Arena, the team is known for passionate fan traditions, including chanting "YES! YES! YES!" after goals.

On rare occasions, fans have even thrown fish onto the ice—a long-running inside joke aimed at their rival, the New York Rangers, and a nod to Long Island's coastal identity.

BUFFALO SABRES

Founded in 1970, the Sabres play at KeyBank Center in Buffalo. They've reached two Stanley Cup finals (1975, 1999) and are famous for their blue and gold colors, iconic charging buffalo logo, and enthusiastic crowd atmosphere.

MAJOR LEAGUE SOCCER (MLS)

NEW YORK CITY FC

Founded in 2013, NYC FC shares Yankee Stadium with the Yankees and has quickly built a loyal following. Known for its electric match-day atmosphere, the team reflects the city's global roots and growing love of soccer.

NEW YORK RED BULLS

The Red Bulls, based in Harrison, New Jersey, were one of MLS's original teams. With a devoted fan base and a soccer-specific stadium—Red Bull Arena—they remain fierce rivals of NYC FC in what's known as the "Hudson River Derby."

WOMEN'S SPORTS

NEW YORK LIBERTY: WNBA PIONEERS

Founded in 1997 as one of the original WNBA teams, the New York Liberty quickly became one of the league's most iconic franchises. They played their first game at Madison Square Garden and are now based at the Barclays Center in Brooklyn. The team's name is a nod to the Statue of Liberty and New York's powerful symbolism of freedom and equality.

GOTHAM FC: WOMEN'S PRO SOCCER IN STYLE

NJ/NY Gotham FC is New York's team in the National Women's Soccer League (NWSL). Originally launched as Sky Blue FC, the team rebranded in 2021 with a bold name inspired by NYC's nickname. They play home games in Harrison, New Jersey, but represent the entire metro region and feature U.S. national team stars and rising talent.

NEW YORK ROLLER DERBY: SKATING WITH ATTITUDE

Gotham Roller Derby, founded in 2003, is one of the country's top flat-track roller derby leagues. The women-led league combines athleticism and theatrical flair, with teams like the Brooklyn Bombshells and Manhattan Mayhem competing in matches that draw passionate local fans.

LADY FIGHTERS IN THE RING

New York has produced top female boxers and MMA fighters, with organizations like the New York State Athletic Commission now fully sanctioning women's bouts. Madison Square Garden has hosted historic women's fights, including the first-ever female main event in 2022 featuring Katie Taylor and Amanda Serrano.

HISTORIC SPORTS MOMENTS

OLYMPIC HISTORY

New York is one of just five U.S. states to have hosted the Olympic Games—and the only state to host the Winter Olympics twice. The village of Lake Placid welcomed the world in 1932 and again in 1980.

The 1980 Games are best remembered for the "Miracle on Ice," when the U.S. men's hockey team stunned the heavily favored Soviet Union in one of the greatest upsets in sports history.

THE "SHOT HEARD 'ROUND THE WORLD"

In 1951, Bobby Thomson of the New York Giants hit a dramatic home run at the Polo Grounds to win the National League pennant over the Brooklyn Dodgers. It's one of the most famous moments in baseball history and was broadcast coast to coast on the radio.

THE FIRST MODERN MARATHON IN AMERICA

The Yonkers Marathon, first held in 1907, is the second-oldest marathon in the U.S. after Boston. It helped popularize long-distance running in the country and is still held annually along the Hudson River.

MUHAMMAD ALI'S "FIGHT OF THE CENTURY"

In 1971, Madison Square Garden hosted the legendary bout between Muhammad Ali and Joe Frazier. It was the first time two undefeated heavyweights fought for the title, and marked a cultural milestone far beyond boxing.

THE BIRTH OF THE NBA DRAFT

The very first NBA Draft took place in 1947 at the BAA head-quarters in New York City, laying the foundation for the modern NBA. That year, Clifton McNeely was selected first overall by the Pittsburgh Ironmen.

NEW YORK'S TENNIS LEGACY

The US Open, held annually at Flushing Meadows in Queens, is one of the four Grand Slam tennis tournaments and attracts over 700,000 fans each year. The tournament moved from

Forest Hills to its current site in 1978 and has hosted some of the sport's most iconic matches.

URBAN SPORTS CULTURE

ROLLER SKATING

Historic rinks like Brooklyn's Empire Roller Disco shaped New York's distinct rollerskating culture, which continues today at parks and skating events

STICKBALL

Known as "poor man's baseball," stickball thrived in New York's crowded streets. Baseball legends like Willie Mays famously played neighborhood stickball games.

STREETBALL

New York's legendary streetball courts like Harlem's Rucker Park and "The Cage" at West 4th Street showcase urban basketball talent and culture.

DOUBLE DUTCH

Competitive Double Dutch jump rope—where two ropes spin in opposite directions while one or more jumpers perform tricks—originated in New York City and grew out of play-ground games in neighborhoods like Harlem and the Bronx.

Double Dutch. Photo by Double Dutch Divas,
CC BY-SA 4.0, via Wikimedia Commons

Some moves are even named after the city itself, including routines called "Brooklyn Bridge" and "Times Square," reflecting the creativity and cultural pride of the communities where the sport developed.

HARLEM GLOBETROTTERS

The Harlem Globetrotters are world-famous for blending elite basketball skills with comedy, trick shots, and acrobatic stunts. Though founded in 1926 and originally based in Chicago, the team adopted the Harlem name to reflect the style and talent associated with New York's Black basketball scene.

Now celebrating 100 years, the Globetrotters have toured internationally and helped spread the popularity of basketball around the globe. Many of their players tower well over six feet tall, adding to the spectacle of spinning balls, impossible passes, and gravity-defying dunks.

OUTDOOR & RECREATIONAL SPORTS

HIKING

With thousands of miles of trails—including the Adirondacks, Catskills, and Finger Lakes—New York is a hiker's paradise, offering diverse experiences for all skill levels.

WINTER SPORTS

New York has more ski areas than any other U.S. state, with over 50 resorts catering to every skill level. Whiteface Mountain near Lake Placid boasts the biggest vertical drop in the East, while Hunter Mountain was one of the nation's pioneers in snowmaking—ensuring fresh powder even in warmer winters.

WATER SPORTS

Surfing, whitewater rafting, sailing, and kayaking are all activities that thrive on New York's rivers, lakes, and coastlines. Long Island beaches offer prime East Coast surfing.

FLY FISHING

The Catskills, birthplace of American fly fishing, continues to draw anglers worldwide to historic rivers. Anglers at Ashokan Reservoir use special long-casting techniques due to boating restrictions.

HORSE RACING

Both Saratoga Race Course and Belmont Park represent horse racing heritage, hosting prestigious races like the Travers Stakes and Belmont Stakes.

AUTO RACING

Watkins Glen International and Oswego Speedway attract racing enthusiasts, featuring iconic NASCAR and dirt track races.

A CRICKET FIELD IN CENTRAL PARK

Long before baseball dominated New York's sports scene, cricket was hugely popular in the city. In fact, Central Park still has a dedicated cricket field on its north side near Harlem Meer. Matches are played there today by local and international teams, reflecting the city's diverse communities.

Cricket clubs were active in New York as early as the mid-1800s, and some historians say cricket may have briefly rivaled baseball as America's favorite bat-and-ball sport.

DID YOU KNOW?

The term "hat trick" wasn't born on the ice—instead it came from the sport of cricket. However, hockey in New York helped give it new life. In 1946, a Manhattan hat store owner offered a free fedora to any Rangers player who scored three goals in a game. The name stuck, and now "hat trick" is used in hockey arenas around the world whenever a player nets three goals in one game, with fans even tossing hats onto the ice to celebrate.

15

FUN FOOD AND DRINK FACTS

New York State's food culture reflects its rich immigrant heritage, innovative culinary traditions, and diverse agricultural landscape. From New York City's iconic pizza to Buffalo's famous wings, every region boasts unique flavors and dishes that tell the state's vibrant story.

ICONIC NEW YORK CITY FOODS

NEW YORK PIZZA

Long before "slice" became a verb, New Yorkers were lining up for thin, foldable pies with crisped crusts. In 1905, Lombardi's in Little Italy became America's first licensed pizzeria, and its coal-oven flavor still sets the standard.

What makes a New York slice special? Many credit the city's mineral-rich tap water, which helps create that chewy-yet-crispy crust. Whether it's a late-night dollar slice or a full pie shared with friends, the rule is simple—fold it, don't fork it. And according to the famous "Pizza Principle," the price of a slice has often matched the cost of a subway ride.

NEW YORK BAGELS

Crisp on the outside and chewy on the inside, New York bagels have become the gold standard. The secret lies in the water. Boiled and baked using New York City tap water, these hand-rolled beauties have the perfect texture. You'll find them on nearly every block, topped with a simple schmear of cream cheese or loaded with lox, tomato, and red onion. Some out-of-state bakeries even go so far as to import New York water just to replicate that one-of-a-kind bite.

SCHMEAR VARIATIONS

Ordering "a bagel with schmear" means cream cheese is involved, but in New York, it can get much more creative than plain. From scallion and garden veggie spreads to sweet options like honey walnut or strawberry, schmears are a serious business. Some shops even offer rotating specials, turning a humble breakfast into a showcase of local flavor.

NEW YORK CHEESECAKE

New York-style cheesecake swaps curds for cream cheese, giving it that dense, rich texture we know today. Credit often goes to Arnold Reuben, who introduced the modern version in the 1920s. Junior's in Brooklyn is the most famous stop, but classic diners and bakeries all over the city serve their own decadent versions.

EGG CREAM

Despite the name, there's no egg and no cream in this classic Brooklyn drink. An egg cream is made with milk, seltzer, and chocolate syrup—whipped together to form a fizzy, frothy treat that tastes like a cross between soda and milkshake. It's best enjoyed fresh, before the head of foam disappears.

WALDORF SALAD

The original Waldorf Salad was served at the grand opening of the Waldorf-Astoria Hotel in 1896. It featured apples, celery, and mayonnaise. Walnuts and grapes were added later, transforming the dish into the sweet, tangy, and crunchy salad served around the world today.

REGIONAL SPECIALTIES BEYOND NYC

GARBAGE PLATE

Garbage Plate from Nick Tahou Hots in Rochester, NY. Photo via Evadb user, Public domain, via Wikimedia Commons

Born at Nick Tahou Hots in Rochester around 1918, the Garbage Plate piles home fries and macaroni salad onto a plate, then layers on your choice of meats, like hamburger or sausage. The whole thing is topped with mustard, onions, and a hearty ladle of spicy meat sauce. It's messy, filling, and famously satisfying—especially after midnight.

BEEF ON WECK

A Buffalo classic, this sandwich features sliced roast beef tucked into a kummelweck roll topped with salt and caraway seeds. Served with horseradish and dipped in au jus, it's the perfect mix of tender, salty, spicy, and juicy. Local pubs often pair it with a cold beer for the full experience.

SPIEDIES

Hailing from Binghamton, spiedies are skewered chunks of marinated meat—chicken, pork, or lamb—grilled and served on soft Italian bread. The vinegar-based marinade is what makes them special. SpiedieFest, held every summer, celebrates this upstate food favorite with music and hot-air balloons along for the ride.

UTICA GREENS

Escarole, garlic, hot peppers, breadcrumbs, and Pecorino Romano come together in this spicy and savory dish. Created by Italian-American cooks in Utica, these greens are often served alongside pasta or sandwiches and have become a local staple.

CHICKEN RIGGIES

Another Utica original, chicken riggies are made with rigatoni pasta—locally nicknamed "riggies"—tossed in a creamy tomato sauce with hot cherry peppers and chunks of chicken. The ridged, tube-shaped pasta traps the spicy, tangy sauce in every bite, making it a beloved comfort food across the Mohawk Valley.

THOUSAND ISLAND DRESSING

This sweet, tangy dressing made from mayo, ketchup, and relish is said to have originated on Heart Island in the Thousand Islands. Created by a fishing guide's wife for a shore dinner, it eventually spread to hotel menus and became a worldwide favorite.

WHITE HOTS

Rochester's answer to the hot dog, white hots are made from pork and veal and flavored with white pepper and mustard seed. Their pale color comes from skipping the smoking process used for red hots. They're served with mustard and onions on a steamed bun and are a must at summer cookouts.

MICHIGANS

In Plattsburgh, a "Michigan" means a steamed hot dog covered in a thick, mildly sweet meat sauce, often topped with mustard and raw onions. Despite the name, the dish is pure North Country and a roadside favorite from spring to fall.

ADIRONDACK PACK BASKET CUISINE

Adirondack guides and settlers cooked with what they carried —think fry bread, trout, wild berries, and venison stew. These rustic, hearty meals reflect the region's self-reliant traditions and are still celebrated at local cookouts and festivals.

BUFFALO WINGS

In 1964, Teressa Bellissimo of Buffalo's Anchor Bar whipped up a late-night snack for her son and his friends using leftover chicken wings. She deep-fried them and tossed them in a tangy cayenne pepper sauce. The result was an instant hit. Today, "Buffalo style" means wings coated in buttery hot sauce and served with celery sticks and bleu cheese dressing to balance the heat.

SWEET TREATS & SNACKS

ICE CREAM SUNDAE

Ithaca claims to be the birthplace of the sundae. In 1892, a soda fountain owner served vanilla ice cream topped with cherry syrup on a Sunday, and the name stuck. Later spelling tweaks gave us the modern "sundae." From hot fudge to rainbow sprinkles, every spoonful is a nostalgic delight.

CRONUT

Cronut - a mashup of a croissant and a doughnut. Photo via depositphotos.com

In 2013, pastry chef Dominique Ansel created the Cronut—a flaky, deep-fried mashup of croissant and doughnut. Fans waited in line for hours just to get one. Today, you can still find seasonal flavors and devoted fans lining the sidewalk outside his SoHo bakery.

POTATO CHIPS

Saratoga Springs gave us one of the world's most addictive snacks. In 1853, chef George Crum sliced potatoes paper-thin, fried them until crisp, and served them as a joke to a fussy customer. They were a hit—and "Saratoga Chips" became the original potato chip.

SPONGE CANDY

Buffalo's sweet secret is sponge candy, a honeycomb-textured confection made by whipping sugar and baking soda into a crunchy puff, then coating it in chocolate. Light, crisp, and melt-in-your-mouth delicious, it's a hometown favorite.

JELL-O

Jell-O was born in LeRoy, New York, in 1897. What began as a powdered gelatin mix became a national icon and inspired its own museum. From wobbly salads to neon-hued desserts, Jell-O remains one of America's jiggliest inventions.

BLACK AND WHITE COOKIE

With its soft, cake-like texture and split icing, the black and white cookie has been a New York staple since the early 1900s. Half vanilla and half chocolate frosting, it's not just a snack but a symbol of local bakery tradition.

HALFMOON COOKIES

Utica's halfmoons are cousins of the black and white cookie, but they're fluffier, domed, and topped with buttercream instead of icing. One side vanilla, one side chocolate, these cake-like treats are a bakery favorite across Central New York.

ENTENMANN'S

Entenmann's began as a family bakery in Brooklyn in 1898. Their iconic crumb-topped coffee cakes and swirl breakfast treats earned them a permanent spot in grocery store aisles across the country—and in countless weekend brunches.

BEVERAGES

MANHATTAN COCKTAIL

The Manhattan was born at the Manhattan Club in the 1870s and became one of the first modern cocktails. A smooth blend of rye or bourbon, sweet vermouth, and bitters, it's always stirred, never shaken. Top it with a cherry and you're sipping on Gilded Age glamour.

FINGER LAKES WINE REGION

Upstate New York's Finger Lakes region is one of the country's top wine destinations. Steep hillsides and deep glacial lakes create the perfect conditions for grapes like Riesling, Pinot Noir, and Gewürztraminer. Take a drive and you'll find vineyard views, tasting rooms, and small-batch wines that rival anything from the West Coast.

GRAPE JUICE

In 1869, Dr. Thomas Welch of Westfield figured out how to stop grape juice from fermenting into wine by pasteurizing it. The result? The world's first commercial grape juice. It was a breakthrough for churches and households alike—and it still fills fridges across America today.

GENESEE CREAM ALE

Brewed in Rochester since 1878, Genesee Cream Ale is a local classic. It's part lager, part ale, and all smooth. With its mild hops and crisp finish, it's a beloved brew across Western New York and a staple at backyard barbecues.

MILK (STATE BEVERAGE)

Milk became New York's official state beverage in 1981, a nod to the state's huge dairy industry. New York ranks near the top in milk production nationwide and is also home to famous dairy brands like Chobani. Whether it's in cheese, ice cream, or yogurt, New York milk makes its mark.

AGRICULTURAL & ARTISANAL FOODS

APPLE VARIETIES

Upstate New York is a powerhouse in apple innovation. Cornell University's orchards developed popular varieties like Empire, Cortland, and Cripps Pink (also known as "Pink Lady"), all bred to stay crisp and withstand cold winters. With more than 600 orchards statewide, New York is second only to Washington in apple production.

MAPLE SYRUP

Every spring, the forests of the Adirondacks come alive with the drip of sap into metal buckets. With over 800,000 gallons produced each year, New York is one of the top maple syrup states in the U.S.—a worthy rival to even Canada. Boiled down in rustic sugar shacks, that sweet, sticky syrup is poured on everything from pancakes to popcorn.

LONG ISLAND DUCK

Once home to dozens of duck farms, Long Island earned its title as the nation's duck capital. The region's Pekin ducks are known for tender meat and mild flavor, especially the prized breast used in confit, roasting, and smoking.

YOGURT

In 2007, a small upstate factory started churning out Chobani Greek yogurt—and transformed New York into a yogurt empire. The state now produces more yogurt than any other in the U.S., earning yogurt the title of "State Snack" in 2014. Thick, tangy, and packed with protein, it's a dairy aisle staple from coast to coast.

CAYUGA BLUE CHEESE

Invented at Cornell in 1941, Cayuga Blue was the first blue cheese in the U.S. made from cow's milk. Aged in caves near Cayuga Lake, its creamy texture and bold tang have earned it national awards and a devoted fan base.

HUDSON VALLEY SHIITAKE MUSHROOMS

In the Hudson Valley, artisan farmers grow shiitake mushrooms the traditional way—by inoculating oak logs with spores. These plump, earthy mushrooms pop up year-round and star in everything from risottos to ramen.

RESTAURANT & FOOD HISTORY

DELMONICO'S

Opened in 1837, Delmonico's helped define American fine

dining. It introduced iconic dishes like Eggs Benedict, Lobster Newberg, and the Delmonico steak. With elegant dining rooms and one of the first public cocktail lounges, Delmonico's showed Americans that restaurant cuisine could be refined and indulgent—not just meat and potatoes.

FRAUNCES TAVERN

Since 1762, this historic Stone Street pub has served food, drinks, and Revolutionary War lore. George Washington bid farewell to his officers here in 1783, making it one of the most significant gathering places in early U.S. history. You can still toast liberty with a pint in the same building where the founding fathers once gathered.

NATHAN'S FAMOUS

In 1916, Polish immigrant Nathan Handwerker started selling hot dogs for a nickel at Coney Island. That humble stand became Nathan's Famous, now a global brand. Every July 4th, its annual hot dog eating contest draws massive crowds and international media attention, proving that even the simplest food can become a cultural phenomenon.

FOOD TRUCK REVOLUTION

New York's sidewalks have always been home to pretzel stands and hot dog carts, but the late 2000s brought a new kind of street food scene. Outfitted with full kitchens and creative menus, more recent gourmet trucks began to serve items like Korean tacos, lobster rolls, churro ice cream sandwiches, and even charcoal-grilled corn dripping in chile-lime butter.

Chef Roy Choi's L.A.-based Kogi BBQ truck helped kick off the nationwide craze, inspiring New York chefs to roll out fusion creations like kimchi quesadillas and banh mi sliders. In

Brooklyn, the weekend market Smorgasburg became a proving ground for food truck fame. Some, like The Halal Guys, built such a loyal following that their carts evolved into full-blown international restaurant chains.

Securing a food truck permit became nearly impossible. With more than 5,000 applicants competing for just 500 new permits between 2010 and 2012, a secondary market emerged where permits were traded like hot commodities. Despite the challenges, many trucks used their platform to support communities—partnering with charities, offering mobile soup kitchens, or launching literacy drives. It wasn't just about street food. It was a full-blown culinary movement.

UNIQUE FOOD STORIES & CURIOSITIES

PIZZA PRINCIPLE

Economists and subway riders alike have long observed that the price of a slice of New York pizza tends to rise in lockstep with subway fares. Known as the Pizza Principle, this quirky correlation has held since the 1960s, making your lunch a surprisingly reliable transit forecast.

THE BAGEL INDEX

It's not just pizza. The average cost of a plain bagel in New York has often mirrored subway fare increases. Some analysts even joke that if a bagel hits three dollars, it's time to brace for another transit hike. Breakfast and your commute, forever linked.

For years, riders compared bagel prices to the cost of a Metro-Card ride. Today, whether you tap with OMNY or remember the swipe era, the bagel-to-subway connection remains a quirky piece of New York economic folklore.

THE BIG MAC–RENT PRINCIPLE

Inspired by The Economist's global Big Mac Index, local researchers noted that the price of a Big Mac in Manhattan often tracks closely with average rent per square foot. If your burger gets more expensive, your apartment might soon follow.

CORNELL CHICKEN

At a 1949 state fair cook-off, Cornell professor Dr. Robert Baker introduced a tangy, vinegar-and-mustard chicken marinade that quickly became a New York classic.

Slathered on chicken quarters and grilled to a golden crisp, his recipe became known as "Cornell Chicken." It's still bottled, barbecued, and beloved at fairs and fundraisers across the state.

MANHATTAN VS. NEW ENGLAND CLAM CHOWDER

In Manhattan, Italian immigrants added tomatoes, carrots, and celery to their seafood stews, creating a red, veggie-packed clam chowder. Up north in New England, colonial cooks preferred a rich cream base and smoky salt pork.

The result? Two iconic chowders—and one ongoing culinary rivalry. From coast to coast, restaurants continue to host "Chowder Showdowns" where fans take sides, one spoonful at a time.

DID YOU KNOW?

The most expensive bagel ever sold was created in New York City, priced at $1,000! Made at the Westin New York, it was topped with white truffle cream cheese and gold flakes, offering a truly extravagant breakfast experience.

16

FAMOUS NEW YORKER INVENTIONS

From skyline-shaping lifts to snack staples and global games, New York inventors or innovators have left their mark on nearly every aspect of modern life. Below, sections group these breakthroughs into themes, each mini-essay telling the back-story behind something we commonly use.

EVERYDAY ESSENTIALS

SAFETY PIN (1849)
Walter Hunt cobbled together a coiled wire fastener to pay off a $15 debt—then sold the patent for $400. His simple spring-clasp design still holds fabric (and ideas) together today.

SEWING MACHINE REVOLUTION (1851)
While sewing machines existed before, it was New Yorker Isaac Merritt Singer who made them practical for everyday use. Born in Pittstown, New York, Singer patented his improved sewing machine in 1851, adding a foot pedal (or "treadle") and a straight needle that made it faster and easier to use.

His design transformed clothing production and home sewing, turning Singer into one of the best-known names in the industry.

TOILET PAPER (1857)

Before toilet paper, people used whatever was available—leaves, corncobs, cloth rags, newspapers, or water—with habits varying widely by region and era. In 1857, Joseph Gayetty introduced one of New York City's most unusual firsts: medicated paper sheets infused with aloe, sold as a more hygienic and soothing alternative.

Marketed as Gayetty's Medicated Paper, the sheets were sold individually in New York pharmacies and even stamped with Gayetty's name. Toilet paper didn't become a household staple until perforated rolls appeared decades later, but the idea was born in New York.

DIXIE CUPS (1907)

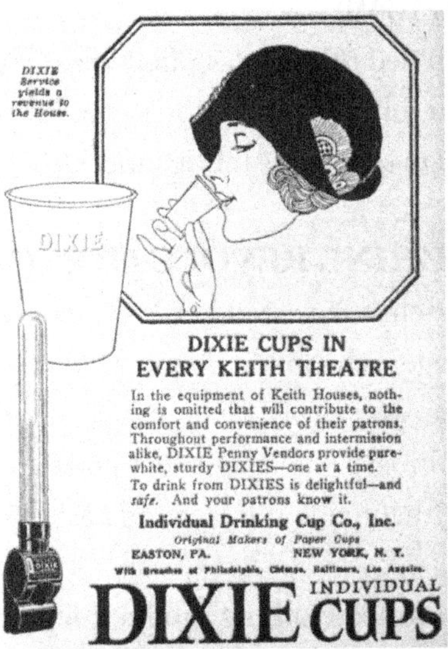

Early Dixie Cup ad. Photo by Individual Drinking Cup Company, Public domain, via Wikimedia Commons

Lawrence Luellen's single-serving paper cups aimed to curb shared germs at public water fountains. "This cup belongs to you" became a household mantra—and helped launch the disposable industry.

Q-TIP COTTON SWAB (1923)

Inspired by watching his wife clean their baby's ears with cotton, Leo Gerstenzang in New York City launched pre-mounted swabs. "Q-Tip" stands for "quality tip"—and it cleaned up hygiene worldwide.

BUILDING & URBAN LIFE

ELEVATOR SAFETY BRAKE (1853)

Elisha Otis of Yonkers amazed crowds at the 1854 World's Fair when he cut the cable on his demonstration elevator. Instead of crashing, the platform stopped in mid-air thanks to his new safety brake. This invention made skyscrapers possible and changed city skylines forever.

ESCALATOR (1899)

Jessup Whitehead patented the first working "revolving staircase," but it was the Otis Elevator Company in New York that brought the idea to life. They built the first commercial escalator at Coney Island in 1909, giving the world its first taste of moving stairs.

AIR CONDITIONING (1902)

Willis Carrier installed the first modern electrical air conditioning unit at a printing plant in Brooklyn. His system was designed to control humidity, but it ended up revolutionizing indoor comfort in homes, offices, and cars.

NEW YORK SUBWAY (1904)

On October 27, 1904, the Interborough Rapid Transit Company opened New York City's first underground subway line. The original route ran from City Hall to 145th Street, traveling north through Manhattan before crossing west at 42nd Street and continuing uptown. The original City Hall station is now closed but still exists beneath Lower Manhattan.

Much of this pioneering line later became part of today's 1 train, while other sections evolved into additional subway routes. The system set the foundation for modern mass transit in New York—and inspired subway systems around the world.

PARKING METER (1935)

Although invented by Gerald Drake of Oklahoma, the parking meter had a big moment in Manhattan. New York's first curb-side meter helped transform how cities manage street parking and urban traffic flow.

MONEY, BANKING & TRANSACTIONS

STOCK TICKER (1867)

Edward Calahan invented the stock ticker to transmit real-time stock prices over telegraph lines. His machine printed out a continuous strip of updates for brokers far from Wall Street. It changed the way markets worked and inspired the famous ticker-tape parades.

CREDIT CARD – CHARG-IT (1946)

In 1946, John Biggins of the Flatbush National Bank created a local charge card called Charg-It to simplify neighborhood purchases. Customers used the card at participating stores, the bank paid the merchants, and customers repaid the bank later.

Charg-It only worked locally, but its bank-centered payment system became the model that later evolved into nationwide credit card networks.

DINERS CLUB CREDIT CARD (1950)

After forgetting his wallet during a business meal, Frank McNamara came up with the idea for a card that could cover dinner on credit. The Diners Club card launched soon after and was accepted at 27 restaurants in Manhattan. It became the prototype for modern credit cards.

AUTOMATED TELLER MACHINE (1969)

On September 2, Chemical Bank in Rockville Centre activated the first ATM in the United States. For the first time, New Yorkers could withdraw cash around the clock without needing a human teller. The idea quickly spread to banks across the country and around the world.

OFFICE & EVERYDAY TECH

TIME CLOCK (1888)

Willard Bundy of Auburn invented the mechanical time clock to record workers' hours on punch cards. It helped standardize payroll and marked the beginning of modern timekeeping in the workplace.

FIRST RADIO AD (1922)

Radio took a big leap on WEAF in New York City when a 10-minute ad promoted an apartment rental. It was the world's first paid radio commercial and helped turn broadcasting into a powerful business.

XEROX (1938)

In a small lab in Astoria, patent attorney Chester Carlson created the first dry copy of a printed page. This process, called xerography, led to the rise of the Xerox Corporation. By 1959, the Xerox 914 made it possible to copy documents with the push of a button, changing office life forever.

REMOTE CONTROL (1955)

Engineer Eugene Polley invented the first wireless TV remote at RCA's lab in Saratoga Springs. Called the Flashmatic, it used a beam of light to change the channel and adjust volume, freeing viewers from having to leave their spot on the couch.

TELEVISION CABLE PREMIUM CHANNEL (1972)

Home Box Office, better known as HBO, began in New York as the first cable channel that required a subscription. It broadcast uncut movies and live events, paving the way for premium television and the streaming platforms we know today.

UPC BARCODE SCAN (1974)

On June 26, at Marsh's supermarket in Troy, New York, a pack of Wrigley's gum became the first item ever scanned with a Universal Product Code. That moment launched the age of barcodes and transformed retail checkout forever.

FOOD & SNACKS

CHEWING GUM (1871)

Thomas Adams of Staten Island experimented with chicle, a natural latex, while searching for a rubber substitute. He realized it made great chewing gum instead. His first product, Adams New York No. 1, helped launch the gum industry.

EGGS BENEDICT (1894)

Delmonico's restaurant in Manhattan is credited with creating the brunch favorite known as Eggs Benedict. The original version featured poached eggs on English muffins with Canadian bacon and hollandaise sauce. It remains a classic today.

CEREAL MASCOTS & MADISON AVENUE (1930s–1960s)

Although many breakfast cereals were invented in Michigan, the characters that made them famous were often created in New York City's advertising agencies. Madison Avenue marketers helped introduce animated cereal mascots like Tony the Tiger, Snap! Crackle! Pop!, and Cap'n Crunch through radio and television commercials.

SPAGHETTI AND MEATBALLS (Early 1900s)

Italian immigrants in New York City paired spaghetti noodles with slow-simmered meatballs and tomato sauce. This mash-up of Italian and American flavors became a signature of Italian-American cuisine.

OREO COOKIE (1912)

The National Biscuit Company introduced the Oreo at its factory in Manhattan's Chelsea neighborhood. Two chocolate wafers and a layer of vanilla cream became America's best-selling cookie and a global dunking icon.

GAMES, TOYS & CHARACTERS

TEDDY BEAR (1902)

After President Theodore Roosevelt famously refused to shoot a tied-up bear cub, Brooklyn shopkeeper Morris Michtom made a stuffed bear in his honor. He displayed it in his candy shop window and called it "Teddy's Bear." The cuddly toy quickly became a national favorite.

CROSSWORD PUZZLE (1913)

Arthur Wynne, an editor at the New York World newspaper, published the first "Word-Cross" puzzle as a Sunday feature. It was an instant hit with readers. Within months, crossword puzzles were a citywide obsession.

MONOPOLY (1935)

Charles Darrow of Philadelphia made Monopoly famous, but the roots go back to a New York-based economist named Elizabeth Magie. She patented a game called "The Landlord's Game" in 1904 to teach lessons about property and capitalism.

SCRABBLE (1938)

Architect Alfred Butts invented a word game while stuck inside during the Great Depression. He studied letter frequencies in the New York Times and created a game called "Criss Cross Words." Renamed Scrabble in 1948, it went on to sell more than 150 million sets worldwide.

BATMAN (1939)

Artist Bob Kane and writer Bill Finger created Batman in a small New York studio. Inspired by the city's shadows, skyscrapers, and alleys, they imagined a masked hero who would become one of the most enduring comic book characters in the world.

MR. POTATO HEAD (1952)

George Lerner, living in Brooklyn, created a toy that let children stick plastic eyes, noses, and mouths into real potatoes. It became the first toy ever advertised on television. A plastic version later made it a household name.

MEDICAL & SAFETY

SMOKE DETECTOR (1890s, conceptual)

Francis Robbins Upton, a partner of Thomas Edison, filed one of the earliest patents for detecting smoke. Although working models came decades later, his design was among the first to imagine automatic fire detection for home safety.

PENICILLIN MASS PRODUCTION (1943)

Alexander Fleming discovered penicillin, but it was Pfizer's plant in Brooklyn that figured out how to make it by the gallon. Using deep-tank fermentation, they turned the antibiotic into a mass-produced lifesaver during World War II and beyond.

IMPLANTABLE PACEMAKER (1958)

While working on a heart monitor in Buffalo, engineer Wilson Greatbatch accidentally inserted the wrong resistor into a circuit. Instead of failing, it sent steady electrical pulses—just what a weakened heart needed. That mistake led to the first implantable pacemaker.

HOME SECURITY SYSTEM (1969)

Marie Van Brittan Brown, a nurse living in Queens, invented the first home security system. Her design included a closed-circuit television camera, a two-way microphone, and a remote-controlled door lock. Today's smart home systems trace back to her blueprint.

SPORTS, GAMES & RECREATION

KNICKERBOCKER BASEBALL RULES (1845)

In Manhattan, Alexander Cartwright and the Knickerbocker Base Ball Club wrote down the first official baseball rules. Their version introduced foul lines, nine-player teams, and nine innings. Those basics still define the game today.

CURVEBALL (1867)

Brooklyn pitcher Candy Cummings figured out how to make a baseball curve mid-air. By snapping his wrist just right, he gave the ball a bend that baffled batters. The curveball soon became a game-changing pitch.

SCUBA GEAR (1939)

In 1939, Christian J. Lambertsen, a physician from New York City, invented an early underwater breathing device he called LARU, short for Lambertsen Amphibious Respiratory Unit.

The U.S. military later adopted and refined his design, renaming the concept SCUBA, an acronym for Self-Contained Underwater Breathing Apparatus. Lambertsen's invention laid the foundation for modern scuba diving and underwater rescue operations.

HIGH FIVE (1977)

At Shea Stadium, Dodgers outfielder Glenn Burke raised his hand to celebrate a home run by teammate Dusty Baker. Baker slapped it, creating a new kind of gesture. That spontaneous moment became the world's favorite celebratory greeting.

DID YOU KNOW?

New York State continues to be a hub of invention and innovation. In 2020 alone, inventors living in New York were granted more than 10,500 U.S. patents, including over 9,300 utility patents for new processes, machines, and technologies.

17

FAMOUS NEW YORKERS

New York has always been a magnet for talent, ambition, and big dreams. From Olympic champions to groundbreaking scientists, from barrier-breaking politicians to legendary performers, the Empire State has produced (and inspired) some of the most remarkable people in history.

ATHLETES

GERTRUDE EDERLE

Born in Manhattan in 1905, Gertrude Ederle was a swimming prodigy who set 29 national records before turning 16. She won gold at the 1924 Olympics, when women's swimming was still new to the Games.

In 1926, she became the first woman to swim across the English Channel—and she beat the men's record by nearly two hours. Ederle helped change how the world viewed women's strength and endurance. She later taught swimming to deaf children and became a quiet advocate for inclusion and opportunity in sport.

ABBY WAMBACH

Born in Rochester, New York, in 1980, Abby Wambach became one of the greatest soccer players in U.S. history. Known for her fearless headers and commanding presence, she scored 184 international goals. At the time of her retirement that was more than any other player, male or female. A two-time Olympic gold medalist and World Cup champion, she's also a bestselling author and a fierce champion for equality in sports and beyond.

MIKE TYSON

Raised in Brooklyn, Mike Tyson became the youngest heavy-weight boxing champion in history at just 20 years old. Nick-named "Iron Mike," he was known for his ferocious power and intimidating presence in the ring. Despite personal and legal struggles, Tyson later reinvented himself as an actor, podcast host, and even a Broadway performer.

SANDY KOUFAX

Brooklyn-born in 1935, Koufax became one of baseball's greatest pitchers, throwing four no-hitters and a perfect game. The left-hander, who was Jewish, famously refused to pitch Game 1 of the 1965 World Series because it fell on Yom Kippur, the holiest day in the Jewish calendar and a day tradi-tionally devoted to fasting and prayer.

The decision made him a cultural icon far beyond baseball. Arthritis forced Koufax to retire at just 30, but he remains the youngest player ever inducted into the Baseball Hall of Fame.

KAREEM ABDUL-JABBAR

Born as Lew Alcindor in Harlem in 1947, he dominated New York City high school basketball before winning three college national championships at UCLA. After converting to Islam and officially changing his name in 1971, Abdul-Jabbar perfected his unstoppable "skyhook" shot in the NBA and scored 38,387 career points, holding the all-time scoring record for 38 years until LeBron James broke it in 2023. Off the court, Abdul-Jabbar is a bestselling author and received the Presidential Medal of Freedom in 2016.

BERNARD KING

Born in Brooklyn in 1956, Bernard King became one of the NBA's most electrifying scorers. His smooth turnaround jumper made him nearly impossible to defend, and he once posted back-to-back 50-point games!

After a serious knee injury that many thought would end his career, he made a remarkable comeback, earning All-Star honors in 1991. His style left a lasting mark on the game and inspired a new generation of players.

MICHAEL JORDAN

Michael Jordan was born in Brooklyn in 1963 but moved to North Carolina at age three. Though his basketball legacy was built in Chicago, his early years in Brooklyn connect him to New York's rich basketball heritage. His Air Jordan brand, launched in 1984, revolutionized athletic footwear and sports marketing.

JACKIE ROBINSON

Born in Georgia but forever tied to Brooklyn, Robinson broke baseball's color barrier in 1947 when he debuted with the Dodgers. He was a four-sport star at UCLA, served as an Army officer, and became a leading civil rights activist after his playing career. His number 42 is retired across all Major League Baseball teams.

PIONEERS AND INNOVATORS

RUTH BADER GINSBURG

Born in Brooklyn in 1933, Ruth Bader Ginsburg grew up in a working-class Jewish family in the Flatbush neighborhood. She graduated at the top of her class from Columbia Law School, all while navigating the deep gender discrimination of the time. As only the second woman appointed to the U.S. Supreme Court, she became famous for her powerful dissents and lifelong fight for equality. Off the bench, she was an opera superfan and once even performed onstage with the Washington National Opera.

JONAS SALK

Born in New York City in 1914, Jonas Salk developed the first successful polio vaccine, which saved millions of lives. Despite the potential for massive profits, he refused to patent it, saying, "Could you patent the sun?" He first tested the vaccine on himself and his family before larger trials led to its release in 1955.

JACQUELINE KENNEDY ONASSIS

Born in Southampton, New York, Jackie Kennedy Onassis was admired for her style, intelligence, and grace as First Lady of the United States. After the White House years, she became a book editor and worked to preserve historic sites. She was also an accomplished equestrian, winning several horse-riding competitions as a child.

ELIZABETH BLACKWELL

Originally from England, Elizabeth Blackwell made history in 1849 when she became the first woman in the United States to earn a medical degree. She later settled in New York, where she opened the New York Infirmary for Women and Children. The clinic offered care to underserved patients and gave other women a rare chance to train as doctors. Her determination helped open the doors of medicine to generations of women who followed.

DAVID SARNOFF

Born in Belarus and raised in New York City, David Sarnoff started out delivering telegrams and then worked his way up through the world of communications. He became a broadcasting pioneer who helped bring radio and television into homes across America. As head of RCA, he built the company into a media giant, launching NBC, the first major broadcast network. His vision helped turn radio and TV from novelties into everyday essentials.

HERMANN BIGGS

Born in Trumansburg, New York in 1859, Hermann Biggs helped shape modern public health in the United States. As New York City's Chief Medical Officer, he pushed for cleaner water, better sanitation, and stronger disease prevention efforts. He established the country's first public health laboratory and introduced mandatory disease reporting, setting a national standard for how cities respond to outbreaks and protect public health.

BENJAMIN N. CARDOZO

Born in New York City in 1870, Benjamin Cardozo became one of the most influential judges in American history. Known for his clear and thoughtful writing, he helped shape how everyday laws work, including rules around contracts, negligence, and personal responsibility. He served on the New York Court of Appeals and later the U.S. Supreme Court, where his decisions continue to influence how justice is delivered today.

BARBARA MCCLINTOCK

Barbara McClintock discovered that genes can move around within DNA—an idea now known as "jumping genes." She first presented this revolutionary finding in 1950, based on research she conducted in the 1940s, fundamentally changing how scientists understand genetic change and adaptation.

Her work was far ahead of its time and largely dismissed for decades. McClintock later conducted research at Cold Spring Harbor Laboratory, where she continued her studies despite skepticism. In 1983, she became the first woman to win the Nobel Prize in Physiology or Medicine without sharing it, cementing her legacy as one of the most influential geneticists in history.

MARGARET SANGER

Born in Corning, New York in 1879, Margaret Sanger was a nurse and activist who became a leading voice for women's reproductive rights. In Brooklyn in 1916, she opened the first birth control clinic in the U.S., where she was arrested for distributing contraceptive information.

Undeterred, Sanger spent her life challenging laws that banned contraception, arguing that women should have the right to control their own bodies. She helped fund early research into birth control pills, and played a pivotal role in making contraception more accessible worldwide by founding what would later become Planned Parenthood.

NIKOLA TESLA

Originally from Serbia, Nikola Tesla spent many of his most productive years in New York City. He worked in Manhattan labs where he developed breakthroughs in alternating current, radio transmission, remote control, and wireless energy—laying the groundwork for much of today's electrical engineering. The modern electric car company Tesla was named in his honor, but he had no connection to it. Elon Musk did not invent the company or the technology; he joined after it was founded.

HARVEY MILK

Born in Woodmere, New York, Harvey Milk became one of the first openly gay elected officials in the United States. As a San Francisco city supervisor, he championed LGBTQ+ rights before his assassination in 1978.

RALPH LAUREN

Born in the Bronx as Ralph Lifshitz in 1939, Ralph Lauren built a global fashion empire with his Polo Ralph Lauren brand, and his classic designs helped define American style for generations.

MARTIN SCORSESE

Born in Queens in 1942 and raised in Manhattan's Little Italy, Martin Scorsese is widely considered one of the most influential directors in film history. Known for gritty, character-driven classics like Taxi Driver, Goodfellas, and The Irishman, his work often explores themes of identity, violence, and redemption—frequently set against the backdrop of New York City.

Scorsese helped revolutionize modern cinema with his bold storytelling, dynamic camera work, and use of popular music. Beyond directing, he's a tireless advocate for film preservation and co-founded The Film Foundation, which has saved over 1,000 films from deterioration.

ACTORS AND ACTRESSES

LUCILLE BALL

Born in Jamestown, New York, Lucille Ball became one of America's most beloved comedians and a trailblazer for women in television. Her groundbreaking sitcom I Love Lucy (1951–1957) was the first to be filmed in front of a live studio audience, and remains one of the most-watched and influential TV shows in history.

Beyond making audiences laugh, she became the first woman to run a major Hollywood studio—Desilu Productions—which produced Star Trek and Mission: Impossible. Jamestown now honors her with the The Lucille Ball Desi Arnaz Museum & Center for Comedy, celebrating her life, comedy legacy, and enduring impact on entertainment.

MARY TYLER MOORE

Before she became America's sweetheart as Mary Richards on The Mary Tyler Moore Show, she was a Brooklyn-born dancer who got her start as the mysterious "Happy Hotpoint" elf in TV appliance commercials. Moore broke barriers for women on television, portraying an independent, career-focused single woman in the 1970s—something revolutionary for sitcoms at the time. Her iconic beret toss in Minneapolis became so famous it was immortalized in a bronze statue downtown.

SIGOURNEY WEAVER

Born in Manhattan, Weaver redefined what it meant to be a female lead in science fiction with her groundbreaking role as Ripley in Alien. Before conquering space monsters, she nearly became a literary scholar, studying English at Stanford and Yale Drama School. Her height—6 feet tall—once made her self-conscious as an actress, but it helped her command the screen as a fierce action hero. She's often called the "Queen of Sci-Fi" thanks to Alien, Ghostbusters, and Avatar.

ANNE HATHAWAY

Born in Brooklyn in 1982, Anne Hathaway began acting in New Jersey theater before breaking out in The Princess Diaries. She later won an Oscar for Les Misérables and is known for films like The Devil Wears Prada and The Dark Knight Rises. Hathaway also serves as a UN Women Goodwill Ambassador.

ROSIE O'DONNELL

Born in Commack, Long Island, Rosie O'Donnell made her mark as a stand-up comic, talk show host, actress, and LGBTQ+ activist. Her 1990s daytime talk show won multiple Emmys, and she later co-hosted The View. Known for her quick wit and big heart, she's also a Broadway producer and fierce advocate for foster care and adoption reform.

WHOOPI GOLDBERG

Born Caryn Elaine Johnson in New York City, Whoopi Goldberg got her start performing in local theater and comedy clubs. She broke out with her one-woman Broadway show, then won an Oscar for Ghost and became one of the few entertainers to win an Emmy, Grammy, Oscar, and Tony.

She was the first Black woman to achieve EGOT status and only the second Black person ever to do so. Before her rise to fame, she worked as a bricklayer and a mortuary cosmetologist —two very down-to-earth New York day jobs. Her wins span comedy, acting, producing, and hosting.

JERRY SEINFELD

Born in Brooklyn in 1954 and raised on Long Island, Jerry Seinfeld co-created and starred in Seinfeld, one of the most influential sitcoms of all time. His clean, observational humor, often drawn from everyday life in New York, made him a stand-up icon. The show was famously "about nothing," but it changed everything in comedy.

PAUL REISER

Raised in New York City, Paul Reiser got his start in stand-up comedy before starring in the hit 1990s sitcom Mad About You, set in Manhattan. His on-screen chemistry with Helen Hunt captured the quirks of married life in the city. Reiser also appeared in major films like Aliens and Whiplash and continues to act, write, and perform.

GARRY MARSHALL

Born in the Bronx in 1934, Garry Marshall was a prolific TV writer, director, and producer who shaped some influential American sitcoms. He created classics like Happy Days, Laverne & Shirley, and Mork & Mindy—all rooted in family, friendship and humor. Later, he directed hit films like Pretty Woman and The Princess Diaries, launching a new generation of stars.

PENNY MARSHALL

Born in the Bronx and younger sister to Garry, Penny Marshall made television history as Laverne in Laverne & Shirley. She broke barriers behind the camera too and became one of the first women to direct a film that grossed over $100 million with Big (1988). Her work in comedy, both on-screen and behind it, paved the way for generations of women in Hollywood.

SPIKE LEE

Though born in Atlanta, Spike Lee grew up in Brooklyn, where his films have deep roots. Movies like Do the Right Thing and Malcolm X transformed how New York City's racial dynamics were portrayed onscreen. He founded 40 Acres and a Mule Filmworks in Brooklyn to produce stories that challenged Hollywood norms.

WOODY ALLEN

Born in the Bronx in 1935, Woody Allen started as a joke writer before becoming a filmmaker. His iconic films like Annie Hall and Manhattan captured the neurotic humor and intellectual vibe of New York City life. He has won multiple Oscars, though his legacy is complicated by personal controversies.

CHRISTOPHER WALKEN

Queens-born in 1943, Christopher Walken began performing at age three and even worked as a lion tamer as a teenager. Known for his unique speaking style, he won an Oscar for The Deer Hunter and has appeared in more than 100 films spanning drama, comedy, and musicals.

AL PACINO

Born in East Harlem and raised in the Bronx, Al Pacino became one of cinema's most legendary actors. With unforgettable roles in The Godfather, Scarface, and Dog Day Afternoon, he brought intensity and depth to every character. He's won an Oscar, two Tonys, and two Emmys—making him one of the few performers to achieve the Triple Crown of Acting.

ROBERT DE NIRO

Born in Manhattan in 1943, Robert De Niro is one of the most respected actors in Hollywood history. He won Academy Awards for The Godfather Part II and Raging Bull and famously collaborated with director Martin Scorsese. After 9/11, he co-founded the Tribeca Film Festival to help revitalize Lower Manhattan. Fun fact: he worked undercover as a real New York taxi driver to prepare for his role in Taxi Driver.

DENZEL WASHINGTON

Raised in Mount Vernon, New York, Denzel Washington is an award-winning actor known for commanding performances in Glory, Training Day, Malcolm X, and Fences. He is also a director and producer who mentors young actors.

TOM CRUISE

Born in Syracuse, New York, in 1962, Tom Cruise became one of the biggest movie stars in the world, known for blockbuster hits like *Top Gun* and the *Mission: Impossible* series. He's famous for doing many of his own stunts, often training for months to pull off high-risk scenes that most actors would leave to professionals.

MUSICIANS

LADY GAGA

Born Stefani Germanotta in Manhattan in 1986, Lady Gaga started performing in New York City clubs as a teenager. She attended NYU's Tisch School of the Arts before dropping out to pursue music full-time. She's one of the few artists to win an Oscar, Grammy, BAFTA, and Golden Globe. Her debut album *The Fame* was inspired by her experiences in New York's Lower East Side music scene.

BARBRA STREISAND

Born in Brooklyn in 1942, Barbra Streisand is one of the few entertainers to achieve EGOT status, having won Emmy, Grammy, Oscar, and Tony awards. She began singing in nightclubs as a teenager while working as a theater usher. Known for her strong creative vision, she even designed a miniature shopping mall in the basement of her home. It includes a vintage clothing store, a candy shop, and an antique store—used purely for decoration and display.

JAY-Z

Born Shawn Carter in Brooklyn's Marcy Houses in 1969, Jay-Z went from selling CDs out of his car to becoming hip-hop's first billionaire. He co-founded Roc-A-Fella Records when no label would sign him, and he's won 24 Grammy Awards. Beyond music, he built a business empire and co-founded the REFORM Alliance to help change the criminal justice system.

LOU REED

Born in Brooklyn in 1942, Lou Reed co-founded The Velvet Underground, which revolutionized rock music with its raw lyrics about New York's underground scene. His solo career, especially the song "Walk on the Wild Side", captured the gritty essence of the city.

BILLY JOEL

Long Island native Billy Joel is one of the best-selling musicians of all time, famously known as the "Piano Man" after his iconic 1973 song. Before committing to music, he trained as a competitive boxer in his teens and even won amateur bouts.

Joel went on to release hit albums like *The Stranger* and *52nd Street*, and he holds the record for the longest-running concert residency at Madison Square Garden, where he has performed dozens of sold-out monthly shows since 2014.

ALICIA KEYS

Born and raised in New York City, Alicia Keys is a singer, songwriter, and pianist known for soulful hits like "Fallin'" and "If I Ain't Got You." She has won multiple Grammy Awards and is also a philanthropist and activist. She graduated as valedictorian of her high school at just 16 years old.

WRITERS

NORMAN MAILER

Born in Long Branch, New Jersey in 1923 but raised in Brooklyn, Norman Mailer gained fame with his World War II novel *The Naked and the Dead* at age 25. He later co-founded The Village Voice, an influential New York City alternative weekly newspaper known for its cultural criticism, investigative journalism, and coverage of arts and politics.

Mailer also helped pioneer "New Journalism," a style that blends literary storytelling with traditional reporting. He won two Pulitzer Prizes for his work.

WALT WHITMAN

Born in West Hills, Long Island in 1819, Walt Whitman became one of America's most influential poets. His groundbreaking collection Leaves of Grass celebrated democracy and everyday life in free verse. During the Civil War, he worked as a volunteer nurse, an experience that shaped his later poetry.

WASHINGTON IRVING

Born in New York City in 1783, Washington Irving became one of America's first internationally celebrated authors. His stories The Legend of Sleepy Hollow and Rip Van Winkle helped define early American literature and remain classics today. Irving also gave New York City one of its most enduring nicknames. He first used the term "Gotham" in an 1807 satire to poke fun at local politics. The name stuck and later inspired Gotham City in the Batman universe.

J.D. SALINGER

Born in New York City in 1919, J.D. Salinger wrote the classic novel The Catcher in the Rye, which captured teenage angst and rebellion. He was famously reclusive after its success. Before becoming an author, he served in World War II and helped liberate a concentration camp.

STAN LEE

Born in New York City in 1922, Stan Lee co-created Marvel

superheroes like Spider-Man, the X-Men, and the Avengers. His storytelling reshaped comic books and pop culture. He once planned to quit comics, but his wife encouraged him to create superheroes the way he wanted—leading to a career breakthrough.

HIDDEN HEROES & UNSUNG FIGURES

ANDREW HASWELL GREEN

Often called the "Father of Greater New York," Andrew Haswell Green was instrumental in consolidating Manhattan, Brooklyn, Queens, the Bronx, and Staten Island into one unified city in 1898. He also helped shape Central Park's design, oversaw the creation of the New York Public Library, and pushed for landmarks like the American Museum of Natural History. Despite his huge impact on the city, his name remains far less known than the projects he made possible.

MADAME C.J. WALKER

Madame C.J. Walker moved to Harlem in the early 1900s and built a groundbreaking beauty empire with products for Black women's hair care. She trained thousands of "Walker Agents" who sold her products door-to-door, creating jobs and empowering women across the country. By the time of her death in 1919, she was one of America's first Black female millionaires and a leading philanthropist in Harlem's community.

AUGUSTUS D. JUILLIARD

Augustus Juilliard made his fortune in textiles and invested heavily in New York's cultural life. In his will, he left $20 million—worth roughly $360 million today—to support the arts, leading to the establishment of The Juilliard School in 1905.

Today, the school is one of the world's most prestigious performing arts conservatories, producing generations of acclaimed musicians, dancers, and actors.

FRANCES PERKINS

Frances Perkins witnessed the horrors of the 1911 Triangle Shirtwaist Factory fire, where 146 workers—mostly young immigrant women—died because of unsafe conditions.

Determined to improve labor standards, she became a leading reformer in New York. Under President Franklin D. Roosevelt she became the first female U.S. Cabinet member. She also helped shape Social Security, child labor laws, and workplace safety standards that are still in place today.

EXTRAORDINARY NEW YORK WOMEN HISTORY FORGOT

EMILY WARREN ROEBLING

When her husband, Brooklyn Bridge Chief Engineer Washington Roebling, became bedridden with decompression sickness in 1872, Emily Warren Roebling took over his duties.

She studied mathematics, engineering, and construction techniques, becoming the bridge's de facto chief engineer for 11 years. Emily managed the daily operations, worked with investors, and became the first person to cross the bridge when it opened in 1883. Her name appears on the dedication plaque alongside the male engineers she worked to support.

ELIZABETH JENNINGS GRAHAM

In 1854, a full century before Rosa Parks, Elizabeth Jennings Graham refused to leave a segregated Manhattan streetcar. When forcibly removed, she sued the transit company and won, with future president Chester A. Arthur as her lawyer. Her legal victory helped end racial segregation on New York City's public transportation. Jennings Graham also founded the first kindergarten for Black children in her home.

JANE JACOBS

Although born in Pennsylvania, Jane Jacobs spent more than 20 years in New York City, where she became one of its most influential activists and urban thinkers. In the 1960s, she led the fight against Robert Moses's plan to bulldoze parts of Greenwich Village to build a highway.

Her landmark book The Death and Life of Great American Cities challenged top-down planning and argued for walkable streets, community input, and preservation. Thanks to her grassroots organizing, neighborhoods like SoHo and the West Village were saved—and modern urban planning was never the same.

MARGARET CORBIN

During the Revolutionary War's 1776 Battle of Fort Washington in northern Manhattan, Margaret Corbin took her husband's place at a cannon after he was killed. She continued firing until she was gravely wounded, becoming the first woman to receive a U.S. military pension. Today, Fort Tryon

Park has a plaque honoring her bravery at the site where she fought.

ADA LOUISE HUXTABLE

Ada Louise Huxtable became the first full-time architecture critic at The New York Times in 1963 and the first person to win the Pulitzer Prize for Criticism. Her writing helped save landmarks like Grand Central Terminal from demolition and sparked America's modern historic preservation movement. She taught New Yorkers to see their city as an architectural treasure worth protecting.

SHIRLEY CHISHOLM

Representing Bedford-Stuyvesant in 1968, Brooklyn-born Shirley Chisholm made history as the first Black woman elected to Congress. In 1972, she became the first Black candidate, and the first woman, to seek the Democratic Party's presidential nomination. Her slogan, "Unbought and Unbossed," reflected her fearless independence. A statue honoring her now stands in Prospect Park.

ALICE AUSTEN

Staten Island photographer Alice Austen captured over 8,000 candid images of everyday New Yorkers between the 1880s and 1930s. She focused on immigrants, street vendors, and working-class life. And her unconventional images documented women's friendships and relationships outside Victorian norms. Her home, Clear Comfort, is now the Alice Austen House Museum.

JACKIE JONES

From 1950 to 1984, Jackie Jones served as a fire lookout in Harriman State Park's forested Hudson Highlands. Her watch-tower, perched 1,276 feet above sea level, helped her protect thousands of acres from devastating wildfires. The Jackie Jones Fire Tower still stands today, offering sweeping views of the Hudson Valley and the Manhattan skyline.

BELLE MOSKOWITZ

In the 1920s, Belle Moskowitz was one of the most powerful women in New York politics, serving as Governor Al Smith's top advisor. She shaped his progressive policies on labor, welfare, and urban reform and even managed his 1928 presidential campaign. Despite her influence, she remains largely absent from history books.

NELLIE BLY

In 1887, investigative journalist Nellie Bly faked insanity to go undercover at the Women's Lunatic Asylum on Blackwell's Island. Her exposé revealed shocking abuse and neglect, sparking mental health reforms. She later gained worldwide fame for circumnavigating the globe in 72 days, beating the fictional record from Around the World in 80 Days.

EMMA LAZARUS

Poet Emma Lazarus, a wealthy Sephardic Jewish New Yorker, wrote The New Colossus in 1883 to raise funds for the Statue of Liberty's pedestal. Her famous lines— "Give me your tired, your poor, your huddled masses yearning to breathe free"— transformed the statue into a symbol of welcome for immigrants. Her words weren't added to the statue until 1903, years after her death.

ZORA NEALE HURSTON

While studying at Columbia University, Zora Neale Hurston documented Harlem Renaissance folklore and African American cultural traditions. Her anthropological work preserved stories that might otherwise have been lost, and her novel *Their Eyes Were Watching God* later became a literary classic.

After her death in 1960, much of her work fell out of print. In the 1970s, author Alice Walker helped revive interest in Hurston's writing, bringing renewed attention to her life and legacy.

ANTONIA PANTOJA

After arriving in New York from Puerto Rico in 1944, Antonia Pantoja founded ASPIRA, an organization that helped thousands of Latino students access higher education. She also won a landmark lawsuit against the NYC Board of Education that established bilingual education programs. In 1996, she received the Presidential Medal of Freedom for her advocacy.

DID YOU KNOW?

In 1977, Martin Scorsese, Robert De Niro, and Liza Minnelli teamed up to make a film titled New York, New York—and while the movie didn't win major awards, its theme song became a global anthem.

When Frank Sinatra covered it two years later, "New York, New York" soared in popularity and is now played at every Yankees home game win, sung at New Year's Eve in Times Square, and belted out by proud New Yorkers everywhere.

18

LIGHTS, CAMERA, NEW YORK!

New York has been the backdrop for some of the most unforgettable moments in film and television history. From the bustling streets of Manhattan to the quiet towns and scenic landscapes of Upstate New York, the state has offered directors a little bit of everything—gritty urban energy, small-town charm, and cinematic views that instantly feel iconic.

MOVIES FILMED IN NEW YORK CITY

BIG (1988)

In this beloved comedy, Tom Hanks plays a 12-year-old boy whose wish to be "big" magically transforms him into an adult overnight. Filmed at iconic New York spots, it features the FAO Schwarz toy store with its giant floor piano, Rye Playland where Josh makes his wish, and a SoHo loft for his adult apartment.

Fun Fact: The giant floor piano scene was filmed inside the real FAO Schwarz toy store on Fifth Avenue. After the movie became famous, the store installed a permanent version so visitors could recreate the scene.

GHOSTBUSTERS (1984)

A team of eccentric scientists turns ghost-catchers in this supernatural comedy filmed across New York City. You'll spot the New York Public Library, Columbia University, and the Hook

& Ladder 8 firehouse in Tribeca, which still serves as a real fire station today.

Fun Fact: Fans continue to visit the firehouse, where the Ghostbusters logo remains painted on the sidewalk outside.

HOME ALONE 2: LOST IN NEW YORK (1992)

Kevin McCallister roams the Big Apple in this holiday favorite, staying at The Plaza Hotel, visiting Central Park, and skating near Rockefeller Center. The famous "Duncan's Toy Chest" is entirely fictional—its exterior was shot in Chicago and the interior was a set.

Fun Fact: Although the real FAO Schwarz briefly appears in a montage, Kevin never actually visits it, despite many fans remembering otherwise.

THE GODFATHER (1972)

This cinematic masterpiece tells the story of the Corleone crime family and was filmed across New York, including Staten Island for the iconic wedding scene. The Corleone home at 110 Longfellow Avenue still looks remarkably similar and is a popular site for movie buffs.

Fun Fact: Marlon Brando's famous cat-stroking moment in the opening scene was completely improvised with a stray cat found on set.

SPIDER-MAN (2002)

Sam Raimi's Spider-Man launched the modern superhero craze, showing Peter Parker swinging past Manhattan's skyscrapers and battling the Green Goblin on New York's streets.

Fun Fact: The upside-down kiss with Mary Jane wasn't nearly as romantic to film—Tobey Maguire was hanging in the rain while water poured up his nose, making it hard to breathe between takes.

MEN IN BLACK (1997)

This sci-fi comedy blends aliens with the chaos of New York City, featuring Battery Park, the Guggenheim Museum, and the New York State Pavilion Observation Towers from the 1964 World's Fair in Queens.

Fun Fact: The Men in Black headquarters is actually the Brooklyn-Battery Tunnel Ventilation Building, whose mysterious art deco look perfectly suited a secret alien agency.

JOHN WICK: CHAPTER 3 – PARABELLUM (2019)

Keanu Reeves races through Times Square, Grand Central Market, and the New York Public Library in this action-packed sequel.

Fun Fact: Reeves trained in martial arts for three months and performed about 90% of his own stunts on location, including the knife fight in Grand Central Market and a horseback chase through Midtown.

THE DARK KNIGHT RISES (2012)

Though Gotham City is fictional, parts of this Batman film were shot in Manhattan, including the Wall Street heist scenes filmed in Lower Manhattan.

Fun Fact: Filming coincided with the Occupy Wall Street protests, unintentionally mirroring the film's themes of social unrest.

I AM LEGEND (2007)

Will Smith wanders an eerily abandoned New York in this post-apocalyptic thriller, filmed at hauntingly empty Washington Square Park, the Brooklyn Bridge, and Times Square.

Fun Fact: The Brooklyn Bridge evacuation scene cost $5 million and took three nights to film, requiring the bridge to close completely and over 1,000 extras to appear as panicked evacuees.

TAXI DRIVER (1976)

Martin Scorsese's gritty classic captures New York's 1970s underbelly with scenes across Times Square, Hell's Kitchen, and the Lower East Side.

Fun Fact: Robert De Niro actually worked 12-hour taxi shifts for a month, driving real passengers to prepare for his role as Travis Bickle.

THE WOLF OF WALL STREET (2013)

This high-energy Scorsese film tells the outrageous true story of stockbroker Jordan Belfort, whose rise and fall on 1990s Wall Street became a symbol of excess and corruption. Scenes were filmed in Lower Manhattan and on Long Island.

Fun Fact: The real Jordan Belfort makes a cameo in the final scene, introducing Leonardo DiCaprio's version of himself at a sales seminar.

DID YOU KNOW?

Although **Wonder (2017)** is set in Manhattan and based on the New York–centered novel by R. J. Palacio, much of the movie was actually filmed in Vancouver, Canada. Thanks to generous tax incentives and flexible filming permits, Vancouver frequently doubles for New York City on screen.

MOVIES FILMED IN UPSTATE NEW YORK

A QUIET PLACE (2018)

This suspenseful thriller starring John Krasinski and Emily Blunt was filmed in the Hudson Valley and Little Falls. Remote bridges and a rural farmhouse created the eerie, sound-sensitive world of the story.

Fun Fact: The crew used hand signals to stay completely silent on set, helping the actors get into the tense atmosphere.

THE PLACE BEYOND THE PINES (2012)

Ryan Gosling and Bradley Cooper star in this crime drama filmed entirely in Schenectady. The title translates the Mohawk word "Schenectady," meaning "beyond the pines."

Fun Fact: Local residents were cast as extras, and real officers from the Schenectady Police Department even appeared on screen.

SALT (2010)

Angelina Jolie plays a CIA agent accused of being a Russian spy, with chase scenes filmed around Albany's Empire State Plaza.

Fun Fact: Jolie performed her own bridge jump stunt onto a moving truck, impressing the film crew and surprising bystanders in downtown Albany.

IRONWEED (1987)

Jack Nicholson and Meryl Streep portray drifters during the Great Depression in this Albany-set drama.

Fun Fact: Nicholson walked the streets of Albany in character to study the lives of homeless residents, adding authenticity to his role.

THE OTHER GUYS (2010)

This buddy-cop comedy shot its explosive car chases in Albany and White Plains, with parts of Empire State Plaza shut down for filming.

Fun Fact: Real cars and pyrotechnics—not CGI—were used for the movie's over-the-top opening crash sequence.

TV SHOWS FILMED IN NEW YORK CITY

ONLY MURDERS IN THE BUILDING (2021–present)

This hit mystery comedy follows three quirky neighbors who start a true-crime podcast to investigate a murder in their building.

Fun Fact: Exterior shots use the real Belnord apartment building, while the intricate interiors are recreated on soundstages in the Bronx.

30 ROCK (2006–2013)

Tina Fey's sharp satire dives into the behind-the-scenes chaos of a fictional sketch comedy show.

Fun Fact: Despite low ratings, NBC kept it on air because executives believed it was one of the best shows they had ever made.

SATURDAY NIGHT LIVE (1975–present)

This iconic sketch comedy show has launched generations of comedians with its live performances from Studio 8H.
Fun Fact: Studio 8H was originally designed for live orchestra broadcasts, giving it the perfect acoustics for the show's legendary musical guests.

FRIENDS (1994–2004)

Six close-knit pals navigate life and love in a hilariously unrealistic Manhattan apartment.
Fun Fact: In reality, that West Village apartment would've been far too expensive for Monica's chef salary, so the show explained it as a rent-controlled sublet.

SEINFELD (1989–1998)

This "show about nothing" follows a neurotic comedian and his eccentric friends as they dissect everyday absurdities.
Fun Fact: The real diner looks nothing like the show's set, but it's doubly famous as the subject of the song "Tom's Diner" by Suzanne Vega.

MAD ABOUT YOU (1992–1999)

This sitcom centers on newlyweds Paul and Jamie Buchman as they juggle love, work, and life in Manhattan.
Fun Fact: The show had crossover episodes with Friends and Seinfeld, placing it firmly in the shared New York sitcom universe of the '90s.

GOSSIP GIRL (2007–2012)

A mysterious blog reveals the scandals of privileged Manhattan prep school teens.
Fun Fact: The school exterior is actually the Museum of the City of New York on Fifth Avenue.

BLUE BLOODS (2010–present)

This family crime drama follows the Reagans, a multi-generational clan of New York City law enforcement officers.

Fun Fact: The food served in those scenes is real, cooked fresh before every take.

SUCCESSION (2018–2023)

This Emmy-winning drama tracks a ruthless media family as they battle for power, prestige, and control of their empire.

Fun Fact: Waystar Royco's "office" is the World Trade Center, and many negotiation scenes were filmed in real NYC hotspots like Cipriani.

LAW & ORDER (1990–present)

A pioneering crime drama that follows detectives and prosecutors as they tackle cases inspired by real events in New York.

Fun Fact: The show's famous "dun dun" sound was created by composer Mike Post by layering unexpected noises—including a slamming jail cell door, an anvil struck with a hammer, drum hits, and even the sound of 100 men stomping on a wooden floor in Japan. The result became one of the most recognizable sound cues in television history.

SEX AND THE CITY (1998–2004)

Sex and the City follows four women as they explore friendship, fashion, and romance in the ever-changing landscape of New York City.

Fun Fact: The exterior of Carrie Bradshaw's apartment is a real townhouse in Greenwich Village. Because so many fans kept sitting on the stoop for photos, the current owners of the building eventually put up a rope and a "No Trespassing" sign to protect their home.

TV SHOWS FILMED IN UPSTATE NEW YORK

ORANGE IS THE NEW BLACK (2013–2019)

This groundbreaking dramedy follows the lives of female inmates in a women's prison and the system that surrounds them.

Fun Fact: Though set in Connecticut, it was filmed at the abandoned Rockland Children's Psychiatric Center in Orangeburg—now a go-to location for other eerie productions.

THE SINNER (2017–2021)

Each season of this psychological crime anthology unravels a new mystery in a quiet town with dark secrets.

Fun Fact: Bear Mountain State Park's Hessian Lake doubled as the fictional town's lake in season one.

BILLIONS (2016–2023)

This high-stakes drama pits a hedge fund billionaire against a relentless U.S. Attorney in a battle of power and money.

Fun Fact: While much of the show takes place in Manhattan, opulent Upstate estates were used to portray the luxurious homes of the ultra-rich.

THE MARVELOUS MRS. MAISEL (2017–2023)

This award-winning period comedy-drama tells the story of a 1950s housewife who reinvents herself as a stand-up comedian.

Fun Fact: Several Upstate locations doubled for 1950s settings, and the "Paris" scenes in season 2 were actually filmed in Manhattan's Lower East Side.

GIRLS (2012–2017)

This coming-of-age dramedy explores the messy lives, friendships, and careers of four young women living in Brooklyn.
Fun Fact: Although mostly filmed in the city, some scenes were shot in real cafés and apartments in Williamsburg and Greenpoint, where locals sometimes wandered into the background.

DID YOU KNOW?

New York State is one of the most filmed places in the world—with over 3,000 films and TV shows shot there every year. From Oscar-winning dramas and iconic sitcoms to horror flicks and superhero blockbusters, directors choose New York not just for its tax incentives, but because no other place captures energy, grit, charm, and scale quite like it.

19

RANDOM & AWESOME NEW YORK

New York State is full of surprises. From Manhattan's hidden architectural marvels to Upstate's natural oddities, the Empire State is brimming with unexpected stories. This collection highlights some of the weird, wonderful, and little-known secrets that make New York one of a kind. Think of it as just a snippet of the countless quirky treasures waiting to be discovered.

NYC SECRETS & HIDDEN SPACES

HIDDEN TENNIS COURTS ABOVE THE MAIN CONCOURSE

Most of the millions of commuters rushing through Grand Central Terminal have no idea that there's a full-sized tennis court just a few floors above their heads.

The Vanderbilt Tennis Club sits on the fourth floor, in a space that once housed an art gallery and even a CBS television studio. You can still book a session today, playing a quiet game high above one of the busiest transit hubs in the world.

A SECRET APARTMENT IN A SKYSCRAPER CROWN

Gold-pyramid roof of the New York Life
Insurance Buidlding. Photo by ButtonwoodTree
at the English-language Wikipedia, CC BY-SA
3.0, via Wikimedia Commons

High atop the gold-pyramid roof of the New York Life Building
hides a secret 3,000-square-foot penthouse built in 1928 for the
company's president. With 360-degree views of Manhattan

and ornate Art Deco detailing, it's been preserved almost exactly as it was nearly a century ago. Today, it's used only for board meetings and private events, and very few photos of this mysterious hidden residence exist.

A SECRET PRESIDENTIAL TRAIN PLATFORM

Beneath the Waldorf Astoria hotel lies Track 61, a hidden railway platform designed for President Franklin D. Roosevelt. It allowed him to discreetly enter and exit New York without revealing his wheelchair to the public. The track included a special freight elevator large enough to lift his entire limousine directly into the hotel. Roosevelt's armored railcar still sits abandoned on the track, and while it's technically inactive, the platform remains connected to the Metro-North system and ready for emergency use.

FUNERAL TRAINS OF THE SUBWAY

From the late 1800s into the early 20th century, New York used special funeral trains to transport the dead from Manhattan to cemeteries in Brooklyn and Queens after new burials were banned on the island.

Rail cars were modified with wider doors to accommodate caskets, and some existing stations near major cemeteries featured separate entrances or platforms to handle funeral processions. As automobiles and hearses became the preferred way to transport the dead, the practice faded by the 1930s—but remnants of these cemetery-adjacent stations can still be glimpsed from today's subway lines if you know where to look.

VERTICAL CEMETERIES OF MANHATTAN

When space ran out for traditional graves in Manhattan, creative burial solutions emerged. In the East Village, the New

York Marble Cemetery and New York City Marble Cemetery use underground marble vaults rather than headstones. At the Cathedral of St. John the Divine, a multi-level columbarium stacks thousands of niches for cremated remains in a vertical cemetery, making the most of the limited space in America's densest borough.

UPSTATE NATURAL WONDERS & ODDITIES

BUFFALO'S ETERNAL FLAME FALLS

In Chestnut Ridge Park near Buffalo, a small waterfall hides a flickering orange flame behind its cascade. Known as Eternal Flame Falls, the mysterious fire is fueled by natural gas seeping from shale rock. Unlike most gas seeps, it stays cool to the touch—baffling scientists. While heavy rain occasionally extinguishes it, visitors often relight the flame, keeping this natural oddity alive.

LAKE GEORGE'S UNDERWATER FOREST

Deep beneath the crystal-clear waters of Lake George lies a sunken forest. Over 300 years ago, a natural dam raised the lake's water level by 30 feet, submerging entire stands of pine trees. Thanks to the cold, oxygen-poor water, the trees remain perfectly preserved and still standing upright. Divers describe the eerie sight as swimming through a ghostly, underwater woodland frozen in time.

THE GRAVITY HILL OF MIDDLESEX

On a quiet road in the Finger Lakes, cars in neutral appear to roll uphill—defying gravity. Known as a "gravity hill," the illusion is caused by the surrounding landscape tricking your eyes into seeing an incline where there's actually a gentle decline. Despite the scientific explanation, locals love spinning spooky tales about magnetic anomalies and wandering spirits.

THE HIDDEN FOREST OF THE ADIRONDACKS

Deep in the Adirondack Mountains lies a 42-acre patch of untouched old-growth forest. Known as "The Big Tree Forest," it contains 400-year-old white pines that reach over 150 feet (45 m) tall and measure 12 feet (3.6 m) around. It escaped 19th-century logging, likely due to a mapping error, and its exact location is kept secret to protect these ancient giants from would-be souvenir hunters.

STRANGE STRUCTURES & ENGINEERING FEATS

THE UPSIDE-DOWN TRAFFIC LIGHT

Syracuse is home to the world's only upside-down traffic light. In the 1920s, the Irish-American residents of Tipperary Hill protested the traditional red-over-green light arrangement, seeing the British "red" as an insult placed above Irish "green."

After repeatedly smashing the standard signal with rocks, the city gave in and installed a green-over-red light in 1928. Today it's a beloved local landmark, complete with a "Stone Throwers" monument honoring the neighborhood's spirited protest.

NEW YORK STATE'S HOLLOW MOUNTAIN

Whiteface Mountain in the Adirondacks hides a remarkable secret. Inside its core is a 427-foot-long tunnel leading to an elevator that carries visitors the final 27 stories to the summit. Completed in 1935, this unusual engineering feat was a pet project of President Franklin D. Roosevelt to make the 4,867-foot peak accessible to people with disabilities like himself.

THE WORLD'S LARGEST KALEIDOSCOPE

In Mount Tremper, you can step inside the world's largest kaleidoscope. Officially recognized by Guinness World Records, this kaleidoscope is built inside a 60-foot-tall grain silo at the Emerson Resort.

It surrounds visitors with a mesmerizing display of shifting colors and patterns projected by giant mirrors. You lie on your back to watch the ever-changing light show, set to music for a fully immersive experience.

THE WINE CELLARS BENEATH BROOKLYN BRIDGE

When the Brooklyn Bridge was built, its massive granite anchorages were found to have hollow chambers. Rather than waste the space, engineers turned them into climate-controlled wine cellars that stayed a constant 60°F (15°C) year-round. From the 1880s until World War I, the cellars stored thousands of bottles of fine wine and champagne. Though sealed today, the chambers still exist inside the bridge's foundations.

HISTORICAL QUIRKS & HIDDEN TALES

BORDER ODDITIES OF NEW YORK

New York's border with Connecticut isn't as straightforward as it looks on a map. A series of colonial-era compromises beginning in 1731 created what became known as the Oblong—a long strip of land along the New York–Connecticut border, sometimes informally described as Connecticut's "panhandle."

As part of this agreement, four small New York exclaves were left completely surrounded by Connecticut. These tiny parcels are commonly described as three enclaves near Greenwich and one near Ridgefield. Although physically cut off from the rest of New York, they remain legally part of New York, meaning residents pay New York taxes and vote in New York elections while relying on nearby Connecticut roads and services.

THE MAN WHO SOLD THE BROOKLYN BRIDGE

In the late 1800s, con artist George C. Parker made a living "selling" the Brooklyn Bridge—sometimes twice a week. He created fake documents and convinced unsuspecting immigrants they could own the bridge and charge tolls. Police often had to stop new "owners" from setting up barricades to collect tolls.

Parker's outrageous scams also included "selling" the Statue of Liberty and Grant's Tomb before he was finally caught and sent to Sing Sing Prison. His schemes became so famous that they helped inspire the phrase "If you believe that, I have a bridge to sell you."

HART ISLAND, AMERICA'S POTTER'S FIELD

Just off the Bronx coast lies Hart Island, the largest public cemetery in the United States. Since 1869, over one million unclaimed or indigent New Yorkers have been buried there in mass graves. For decades, inmates from Rikers Island performed the burials, often laying hundreds of coffins at a time. Recently, the island was transferred to NYC Parks and is slowly being opened to families and the public as both a memorial and nature preserve.

BROOKLYN'S WILD PARROTS

Green-Wood Cemetery in Brooklyn is home to a thriving colony of bright green Monk parrots. Originally from Argentina, these birds escaped from JFK Airport in the 1960s and adapted to New York's harsh winters by building massive communal nests that generate enough heat to survive. Today, the parrots have become a beloved local curiosity, with satellite colonies popping up in other Brooklyn neighborhoods.

DID YOU KNOW?

New York State has more ghost towns than any other state in the Northeast. From abandoned 19th-century canal villages to forgotten Adirondack mining settlements, these eerie remnants of the past are scattered across the state.

20

DIFFICULT HISTORIES OF NEW YORK

Acknowledging Hard Truths

While this book is filled with fun and fascinating facts about New York, it's also important to recognize the state's more difficult histories. From the displacement of Indigenous peoples and the legacy of slavery to struggles for LGBTQ+ rights and the tragedy of 9/11, New York's past includes moments of injustice and heartbreak alongside resilience and progress.

As a white author, I approach these topics with humility, knowing this is not a complete account. My goal is to offer a brief reflection that honors those who endured injustice, highlights the courage of those who fought for equality, and recognizes the communities still working toward a better future.

THE DISPLACEMENT OF INDIGENOUS PEOPLES

Long before European colonization, the Haudenosaunee (Iroquois Confederacy), Lenape, Mahican, and many other Indigenous nations called this land home. Colonization brought forced displacement, broken treaties, and violence.

The Treaty of Fort Stanwix (1768) took vast tracts of Haudenosaunee land, and the Sullivan-Clinton Campaign (1779) during the Revolutionary War destroyed Indigenous villages in central and western New York, driving thousands from their homes.

Today, the Onondaga, Seneca, Mohawk, Cayuga, Oneida, and Tuscarora nations continue to fight for sovereignty and the return of stolen lands, preserving their languages, cultures, and traditions despite centuries of hardship.

SLAVERY IN NEW YORK

Though often thought of as a "free" Northern state, New York actively participated in slavery for more than two centuries. Enslaved Africans worked on farms, in homes, and in businesses across the state, with New York City serving as a major hub for the transatlantic slave trade in the 1600s and 1700s. By 1790, New York had the largest enslaved population in the North.

In 1799, New York began gradual emancipation, freeing children born to enslaved mothers only after they reached adulthood. Full abolition didn't come until July 4, 1827, and even after emancipation, systemic racism and segregation shaped the lives of free Black communities for generations.

NEW YORK CITY'S SLAVE MARKET

In the early 1700s, New York City operated a major slave market at Wall Street and Pearl Street, where enslaved men, women, and children were bought and sold. This market was central to the city's economy, fueling its growth while enriching merchants.

A small plaque now marks the site, but many visitors (and even lifelong New Yorkers) don't know that Wall Street's financial history is tied directly to the buying and selling of human lives.

ANTI-IMMIGRANT DISCRIMINATION

New York has long been a gateway for immigrants seeking opportunity, but it also has a history of hostility toward newcomers. Irish and Italian immigrants in the 19th century faced xenophobia, and were often denied housing and work. In the 20th century, Asian immigrants faced discriminatory laws, including bans on property ownership and employment restrictions.

While today New York celebrates its diversity, these struggles remind us that inclusion was not always guaranteed—it was fought for over generations.

LGBTQ+ DISCRIMINATION AND RESILIENCE

New York City is now seen as a global symbol of LGBTQ+ pride, but for much of its history, queer communities faced harassment and violence. Until the 1970s, police regularly raided gay bars and arrested patrons, outing them publicly and costing many their jobs and families.

Everything changed with the Stonewall Uprising of 1969, when LGBTQ+ New Yorkers fought back against a police raid at the Stonewall Inn in Greenwich Village. This act of resistance sparked the modern LGBTQ+ rights movement, leading to Pride marches and decades of activism that continue today.

THE FIRST PRIDE MARCH

On June 28, 1970, New York City hosted the first-ever Pride march, then called the Christopher Street Liberation Day March. The march began at the Stonewall Inn and stretched up Sixth Avenue, blending protest with celebration and demanding visibility and equality for LGBTQ+ people.

What started as a grassroots demonstration has since grown into a global movement. Today, New York's Pride March draws millions each June, honoring those who fought for equality and continuing the call for justice worldwide.

URBAN RENEWAL & DISPLACEMENT

In the mid-20th century, so-called "urban renewal" projects reshaped New York City, often at the expense of poor and working-class communities. The construction of the Cross Bronx Expressway, for example, displaced thousands of families and destroyed vibrant neighborhoods, deepening racial and economic divides.

Similar projects across the state uprooted communities in the name of "progress," leaving lasting scars and contributing to cycles of poverty and inequality.

CIVIL RIGHTS STRUGGLES IN NEW YORK

Even in the North, racial inequality persisted long after slavery ended. In 1964, the Harlem Riots erupted in response to police brutality, echoing the frustration and anger of many Black communities facing discrimination in housing, education, and employment.

While New York also produced powerful civil rights leaders, including Malcolm X and Shirley Chisholm, the fight for racial justice here has been ongoing, reminding us that progress is never simple or complete.

SEPTEMBER 11, 2001

One of New York's darkest days was September 11, 2001, when terrorist attacks destroyed the Twin Towers of the World Trade Center. Nearly 3,000 people lost their lives, including first responders who rushed into danger to save others. The attacks left deep emotional and physical scars on survivors, rescue workers, and the city as a whole.

In the aftermath, support poured in from across the country and around the world—including an extraordinary act of kindness from Canada. When U.S. airspace was closed, Canada welcomed more than 33,000 stranded travelers in an operation called Operation Yellow Ribbon. The small town of Gander, Newfoundland, famously opened its homes to over 6,500 unexpected guests, offering food, shelter, and compassion during a time of fear and uncertainty.

Today, the 9/11 Memorial & Museum at Ground Zero honors the lives lost and stands as a testament to resilience, remembrance, and unity.

REFLECTION

These histories do not define all of New York, but they are an essential part of its story. Remembering them honors the strength of those who endured injustice, the communities who fought back, and the allies—near and far—who offered support in times of crisis. By acknowledging these difficult histories, we gain a deeper understanding of the Empire State and the people who have created it, for better and for worse.

21

INTERESTING WAR HISTORY

New York has been a battlefield, a strategic hub, and a home front in nearly every major American conflict. From Revolutionary War chains stretched across the Hudson River to Cold War missile sites hidden in plain sight, the Empire State's war history is full of surprising twists. These stories highlight how New York shaped—and was shaped by—wars big and small.

REVOLUTIONARY WAR (1775–1783)

The Revolutionary War was America's fight for independence from Great Britain, sparked by colonial resistance to British taxes and rule.

THE BATTLE OF SARATOGA: TURNING POINT

In 1777, the American victory at the Battle of Saratoga in upstate New York changed the course of the Revolutionary War. British General John Burgoyne surrendered his entire army of nearly 6,000 men, convincing France to officially join the war as an American ally. This transformed the rebellion into a global conflict and made Saratoga one of the most important battlefields in the nation's history.

BENEDICT ARNOLD'S BETRAYAL

Before becoming America's most infamous traitor, Benedict Arnold was a celebrated hero at Saratoga. But in 1780, while commanding West Point, Arnold secretly plotted to hand the fortress to the British for money and a military commission. The plan fell apart when his British contact, Major John André, was captured with incriminating documents.

Arnold escaped to British lines, but André was captured and later executed as a spy in Tappan, New York. He is believed to have been held at the Old '76 House tavern—built in 1754 and still operating today as one of America's oldest restaurants.

THE GREAT CHAIN ACROSS THE HUDSON

To stop British warships from sailing up the Hudson River, American forces installed an enormous iron chain across the river at West Point in 1778. Each link weighed over 100 pounds, and the entire chain stretched 1,700 feet, creating a floating barrier supported by wooden rafts. The British never attempted to breach it, making this unusual engineering project a quiet but critical Revolutionary War success.

THE CITY THAT REFUSED TO SURRENDER

When British troops sailed up the Hudson in 1777 and demanded the surrender of Kingston, which was at the time New York's temporary capital, the townspeople refused. In retaliation, the British burned the entire city. But Kingston's citizens quickly rebuilt, and the town's defiance became a symbol of Revolutionary resilience that is still remembered every October during "Burning of Kingston" commemorations.

DID YOU KNOW?

During the Revolutionary War, British forces actually occupied New York City for seven years—longer than they held any other American city. When they finally left in 1783, George Washington triumphantly returned to the city in what became known as "Evacuation Day," a celebration that rivaled the Fourth of July for decades afterward.

WAR OF 1812 (1812–1815)

The War of 1812 was fought between the United States and Great Britain over trade restrictions, impressment of American sailors, and British support for Native American resistance.

NEW YORK: THE MAJOR BATTLEGROUND

New York experienced more battles during the War of 1812 than any other U.S. state, largely because of its long border with British-controlled Canada. Communities from Sackets Harbor to Buffalo were repeatedly attacked, occupied, or destroyed.

In December 1813, American forces burned the Canadian town of Newark (now Niagara-on-the-Lake), leaving British civilians homeless at the onset of winter. In retaliation, British troops crossed the Niagara River and burned Buffalo, destroying much of the town and forcing hundreds of New Yorkers from their homes. These back-and-forth raids made the New York–Canada border one of the war's most devastating fronts.

THE BATTLE OF PLATTSBURGH

In September 1814, American forces won a stunning victory at Plattsburgh on Lake Champlain. Despite being outnumbered, the U.S. Navy defeated a British fleet while land forces repelled an invasion of 11,000 soldiers. This battle, paired with the defense of Baltimore, helped force peace negotiations that ended the war.

DEFENSIVE STRONGHOLDS

The fear of British attack led to a wave of fort-building across New York. Castle Clinton, then called West Battery, was constructed off the southern tip of Manhattan to guard New York Harbor. Other forts, like Fort Ontario in Oswego, still stand today as reminders of how seriously New Yorkers prepared for war.

THE CIVIL WAR (1861–1865)

The Civil War was fought between the Union (North) and the Confederacy (South) over slavery, states' rights, and the future of the nation.

THE DRAFT RIOTS

In July 1863, New York City erupted in the deadliest civil disturbance in U.S. history, when a federal draft lottery sparked days of rioting. Angry mobs attacked government buildings, burned homes, and targeted Black residents, whom they blamed for the war. Federal troops fresh from Gettysburg were sent to restore order. At least 120 people were killed, and damages topped $1.5 million—equivalent to tens of millions today.

THE FIRST FEMALE CIVIL WAR SURGEON

Dr. Mary Edwards Walker of Oswego became the first female surgeon in the U.S. Army during the Civil War. She served on the frontlines, was captured as a prisoner of war, and later became the only woman ever awarded the Medal of Honor. Though the medal was controversially rescinded decades later, it was reinstated in 1977, cementing her legacy as a trailblazing physician and soldier.

NEW YORK'S MASSIVE CONTRIBUTION

New York sent more soldiers to fight for the Union—over 450,000—than any other state. Nearly one in three were killed or wounded. Beyond manpower, New York's banks and factories supplied huge amounts of money, weapons, and supplies that kept the Union war effort alive. Yet, New York City also harbored strong Confederate sympathies due to its deep financial ties to Southern cotton.

WORLD WAR I (1917–1918)

World War I was a global conflict sparked by alliances, imperialism, and the assassination of Austria-Hungary heir Archduke Franz Ferdinand, drawing the United States into Europe's "Great War."

NEW YORK'S FIGHTING 69TH

The 69th Infantry Regiment, nicknamed the "Fighting 69th," was a mostly Irish-American unit from New York that became one of the most decorated American regiments in World War I. Their chaplain, Father Francis Duffy, was so beloved for his courage under fire that a statue of him now stands in Times Square.

CAMP UPTON AND IRVING BERLIN

Camp Upton on Long Island trained thousands of soldiers heading to France. While stationed there, Army private Irving Berlin wrote a musical revue called "Yip, Yip, Yaphank" to raise money for the camp. He even drafted an early version of "God Bless America," though it wouldn't be released until decades later.

HARLEM HELLFIGHTERS

The 369th Infantry Regiment was an African American unit from New York that served under French command due to segregation in the U.S. military. They spent more time in combat than any other American regiment and never lost a man to capture.

The entire unit was awarded France's highest military honor, the Croix de Guerre. The regiment called themselves the Harlem Rattlers, but when the Germans called them "Hollenkampfer," meaning "Hellfighter," they became known as the Harlem Hellfighters.

WORLD WAR II (1939–1945)

World War II was a global conflict between the Axis powers—
led by Nazi Germany, Japan, and Italy—and the Allies,
including the U.S., Britain, and the Soviet Union. It was driven
by fascist expansion and genocide, resulting in the Holocaust,
massive destruction, and the Allied victory that reshaped the
modern world.

OPERATION PASTORIUS: NAZI SABOTEURS IN NEW YORK

In June 1942, four Nazi agents landed by submarine on Long
Island near Amagansett as part of Operation Pastorius, a
German plan to sabotage American industry during World
War II. Carrying explosives and with plans to attack factories,
railroads, and power facilities, the group was unexpectedly
discovered by a U.S. Coast Guardsman on the beach—setting
off an FBI investigation.

Unbeknownst to the public at first, four additional agents had
landed separately in Florida, bringing the total to eight sabo-
teurs. The mission collapsed when two of the men voluntarily
contacted U.S. authorities, revealing the full plot. All eight
were captured and tried by a military tribunal. Six were
executed, while the two cooperators received prison
sentences.

THE BROOKLYN NAVY YARD

At the height of World War II, the Brooklyn Navy Yard
employed 70,000 workers around the clock building battle-
ships, aircraft carriers, and destroyers. The U.S.S. Missouri, the
battleship on which Japan officially surrendered WWII, was

built in the Brooklyn Navy Yard. It was also the first U.S. shipyard to employ women workers in large numbers.

FORT ONTARIO REFUGEE SHELTER

In 1944, Fort Ontario in Oswego, NY became the only refugee shelter for Holocaust survivors allowed into the U.S. during the war. Nearly 1,000 mostly Jewish refugees lived at the fort under "guest" status until the war ended. Today, it's a historic site and museum honoring this safe haven.

DID YOU KNOW?

During World War II, more than 1.3 million American soldiers passed through Camp Shanks in Orangeburg, Rockland County, New York, before shipping out to Europe. Nicknamed "Last Stop USA," it was the final place many soldiers stood on American soil before heading to war. Today, the Camp Shanks Museum in Orangeburg preserves the memory of the camp and the troops who passed through it.

COLD WAR (1947–1991)

The Cold War was a period of tension between the United States and Soviet Union, marked by nuclear weapons, espionage, and proxy wars rather than direct combat.

GRIFFISS AIR FORCE BASE AND THE NUCLEAR ARSENAL

Griffiss Air Force Base in Rome, New York, played a crucial

role in America's nuclear deterrent strategy during the Cold War. As a Strategic Air Command base, it housed B-52 bombers capable of delivering nuclear weapons anywhere in the world. The base was also home to the Rome Air Development Center, which pioneered advances in radar and early-warning systems.

Though the base closed in 1995, parts of it now serve as Griffiss International Airport and a technology park.

THE SENECA ARMY DEPOT'S WHITE DEER

The Seneca Army Depot near Romulus stored nuclear weapons and other munitions during the Cold War, but it also accidentally created one of New York's most unique wildlife populations. Inside its 10,600-acre high-security fence, a population of white deer—carrying a rare recessive gene—was protected from predators and hunters. Over time, they became the largest group of white deer in the world.

Today, the site is preserved as a nature and historical park, where visitors can still spot these ghostly creatures roaming the fields.

THE NIKE MISSILE PROGRAM

During the height of the Cold War, New York City was encircled by Nike missile sites, part of a U.S. air-defense system designed to intercept Soviet bombers. The name "Nike" refers to the Greek goddess of victory, not the shoe company.

Sites in Queens, Staten Island, and the Hudson Valley housed Nike Ajax missiles and later Nike Hercules missiles, some of which were capable of carrying nuclear warheads.

Although never used in combat, these missiles stood on constant alert until the 1970s, when the rise of intercontinental ballistic missiles made them obsolete. Today, many former missile bases have been transformed into parks and nature preserves.

NEW YORK DURING THE CUBAN MISSILE CRISIS

In October 1962, the Cuban Missile Crisis pushed the world to the brink of nuclear war, and New York City was one of the Soviet Union's top targets. Missiles based in Cuba could have hit the city in fewer than 15 minutes. Fallout shelter signs appeared on public buildings, civil defense sirens were tested, and residents scrambled to stockpile food and water. Though the standoff ended peacefully, those tense 13 days left New Yorkers with a haunting awareness that their city could have been wiped out in moments.

DID YOU KNOW?

One of the Cold War's strangest structures still stands in Manhattan. The AT&T Long Lines Building at 33 Thomas Street was built as a hardened telecommunications hub that could survive a nuclear blast.

Completely windowless, it has its own generators, and enough food and water supplies to keep 1,500 people alive for two weeks after an attack. It remains an active telecom site today, shrouded in mystery and rumored to be linked to secret intelligence operations.

KOREA, VIETNAM, AND BEYOND

These Cold War–era conflicts pitted the U.S. and its allies against communist forces in Korea and Vietnam, followed decades later by the post-9/11 Global War on Terror.

THE NIAGARA FALLS POWER CRISIS

The Korean War's industrial demands caused a major power shortage in Niagara Falls, which supplied electricity to key U.S. defense plants. The crisis led to the creation of the Niagara Power Project, completed in 1961 as one of the world's largest hydroelectric plants.

THE EMPIRE STATE'S TOLL

New York lost more residents in the Vietnam War than any other state—4,120 in total. The New York State Vietnam Memorial in Albany honors their sacrifice with a timeline of the war and the names of every New Yorker who died. In lower Manhattan, a haunting glass-block memorial features letters written by soldiers.

9/11 AND AMERICA'S LONGEST WAR

After the September 11, 2001 attacks destroyed the World Trade Center, thousands of New Yorkers enlisted to fight in Afghanistan and Iraq. Over the next two decades, hundreds of service members from the state were killed in action, linking the memory of 9/11 directly to America's longest war.

FORT DRUM: AMERICA'S MODERN WARRIOR FACTORY

Fort Drum near Watertown is home to the 10th Mountain Division, one of the most deployed units in modern U.S. military history. It played a vital role in the wars in Afghanistan and Iraq, and remains the largest military base in the Northeast.

DID YOU KNOW?

New York has played a pivotal role in nearly every major American conflict, from the Revolutionary War to the Global War on Terror. More than 1.2 million New Yorkers have served in the U.S. armed forces, and the state has contributed more soldiers, supplies, and financial support to America's wars than any other state.

Even today, New York remains one of the nation's most important military hubs, with active installations like Fort Drum and historic sites stretching from Manhattan to the Adirondacks.

22

HOW TO SPOT A TRUE NEW YORKER

New Yorkers are instantly recognizable not by their clothes or even their accents, but by their habits. Whether in the city or upstate, they share an unspoken cultural code that makes them stand out. Some were born here, others moved here and adapted, but all true New Yorkers carry the same set of quirks. Some of these habits are born on crowded city sidewalks, while others stretch across the entire state. Here's how to tell if someone belongs to the Empire State tribe.

A TRUE NEW YORKER (IN THE CITY) WALKS LIKE THEY HAVE SOMEWHERE TO BE

In New York City, walking fast isn't rude—it's expected. Sidewalks function like moving lanes, and stopping suddenly is considered a minor social offense. Locals weave smoothly around slower walkers and tourists, often without breaking stride. Stand still in the middle of the sidewalk and you'll feel it immediately: in the city, sidewalks are for moving, not lingering.

A TRUE NEW YORKER MEASURES DISTANCE IN TIME

If you ask how far something is, they never answer in miles. True New Yorkers always measure in minutes. "Twenty minutes away" could mean a five-block walk in Midtown, or it could be considered part of a 45-minute drive out of the city, which upstate residents casually consider "just down the road."

A TRUE NEW YORKER DOESN'T FLINCH AT CELEBRITY SIGHTINGS

You'll know they're local when they barely glance at a famous actor waiting in line for coffee. They might give the classic celebrity side-eye, just enough to confirm it's really them, but they won't ask for a photo or make a scene. Casual comments like "Oh, I saw Paul Rudd on the subway this morning" are delivered with the same tone as a weather update.

A TRUE NEW YORKER HAS STRONG BAGEL OPINIONS

They'll tell you exactly where to find the best bagel and dismiss out-of-state bagels with dramatic disgust. Expect passionate theories about New York water, boiling methods, and proper hand-rolling. Even transplants who've been here long enough adopt the same intensity because bagels in New York aren't just breakfast—they're part of the culture.

A TRUE NEW YORKER IS NEVER FAR FROM A PIZZA DEBATE

Ask where to find the best pizza and sparks will fly. Someone will argue for a classic Manhattan slice. Another will insist on Sicilian squares or Long Island grandma pies. Someone else will swear Buffalo-style is underrated. Any mention of "New York-style pizza" guarantees at least three people will interrupt with "Actually..." before defending their neighborhood favorite.

A TRUE NEW YORKER HAS MASTERED THE ART OF AGGRESSIVE WAITING

Lines in New York aren't passive. Locals hold their spot with subtle body angles and a forward lean while keeping a sharp eye out for line-cutters. They might scroll on their phone, but don't be fooled—they know exactly who is behind them and will call out anyone trying to skip.

A TRUE NEW YORKER GETS EMOTIONAL ABOUT A GROCERY STORE

Mention Wegmans, Fairway, or Zabar's and you'll hear an enthusiastic monologue. Upstaters will drive 45 minutes just to shop at Wegmans. City dwellers mourn the closing of their favorite bodegas. When a new Trader Joe's opens, it becomes a neighborhood event, celebrated by some and lamented by others who fear it will change the area's character.

A TRUE NEW YORKER HAS MULTIPLE WEATHER VOICES

Winter comes with a resigned tone: "Yeah, we're getting two feet overnight." Spring gets a skeptical voice: "Don't get too excited, it'll snow again in April." Summer is filled with complaints about humidity. Fall is spoken about with genuine reverence: "Just look at these colors."

A TRUE NEW YORKER (IN THE CITY) DOESN'T WAIT FOR WALK SIGNALS

Crossing the street in New York City isn't about traffic lights— it's about instinct and timing. Locals instantly calculate vehicle speed, distance, and urgency before stepping into the street. Tourists hover awkwardly at curbs, while seasoned New Yorkers stride across even before the light changes.

A TRUE NEW YORKER GIVES DIRECTIONS USING GHOST BUSINESSES

When asked for directions, they'll say things like "It's where the old Woolworth's used to be," or "Turn left after what used to be Kim's Video." The landmarks they mention may have closed decades ago, but the mental map of the city exists in layers of past and present that only locals understand.

A TRUE NEW YORKER KNOWS THE BODEGA CAT

They don't just know which bodega makes the best bacon-egg-and-cheese breakfast sandwhich, they are also familiar with the resident cat's name. They'll show you photos, tell you about the cat's quirks, and maybe even warn you about the one that likes to swat at ankles. These cats are treated like neighborhood royalty.

A TRUE NEW YORKER (IN THE CITY) HAS PERFECT SUBWAY BALANCE

City locals can stand in a moving subway car without holding onto anything. Feet planted, knees slightly bent, they scroll, read, or even apply makeup without tipping over during sudden stops. It's a skill learned through repetition—and sudden braking.

A TRUE NEW YORKER ROTATES THEIR CLOSET WITH THE SEASONS

Tiny apartments force locals to migrate wardrobes twice a year. Winter clothes get shoved into storage in April, only to be dragged out again in October with plenty of grumbling about having "no space for all this stuff." Forgotten sweaters and coats reappear like surprise gifts during this ritual.

A TRUE NEW YORKER LIVES BY ALTERNATE SIDE PARKING

Owning a car in the city means structuring your life around street cleaning schedules. Residents wake at dawn, double-park in temporary "holding zones," and form fleeting friendships with neighbors they only see during these early morning rituals.

A TRUE NEW YORKER SPEAKS IN REGIONAL FOOD CODE

Order a beef on weck? You're from Buffalo. Mention spiedies? That's the Southern Tier. Call a soft drink "pop"? Definitely upstate. Talk about egg creams with zero eggs or cream? That's pure NYC. Regional dishes are more than meals—they're identity markers.

A TRUE NEW YORKER HAS EXTREMELY SPECIFIC MENTAL MAPS

They know which subway car doors line up with the exit, which street corners smell worst in summer, and which public bathrooms can be accessed without buying anything. Upstate, they know the gas station with the shortest lines and the one shady parking spot at the county fair.

A TRUE NEW YORKER IS NOISE-PROOF

Sirens, construction, and late-night garbage trucks don't even register. In the city, locals can sleep through a jackhammer. Upstate, residents shrug off lake-effect thunder or train horns. If someone doesn't even look up at a sudden loud noise, they're probably a local.

A TRUE NEW YORKER KNOWS WHAT "UPSTATE" REALLY MEANS

Ask three different New Yorkers where "Upstate" begins and you'll get three different answers. Some say just past the Bronx. Others say north of Westchester. Someone from Buffalo will insist anything south of Albany doesn't count as Upstate at all. Only a true New Yorker can explain these invisible borders.

23

ONLY IN NEW YORK

Every place has its quirks, but New York elevates the unusual to an art form. From occupations that exist nowhere else to foods you'll only find within state lines, the Empire State is home to countless oddities that make it truly one of a kind.

UNIQUE NEW YORK JOBS

ELEVATOR OPERATORS

While automatic elevators have replaced human operators almost everywhere, New York City remains one of the last strongholds of this nearly extinct profession. In Manhattan's most prestigious buildings along Fifth Avenue and Central Park West, uniformed operators don't just press buttons.

They greet residents by name, hold packages, relay messages, and provide security. Some have served the same buildings for decades, becoming beloved fixtures of their neighborhoods.

Elevator operator. Photo by Subway Rat, CC BY-SA 4.0, via Wikimedia Commons

BROADWAY STANDBYS

Unlike understudies who usually perform in the ensemble, Broadway standbys are hired exclusively to wait in the wings, ready to take the stage if a star can't perform. They may learn multiple roles and spend months or even years fully prepared without ever performing. Despite rarely being seen, standbys often earn full Broadway salaries, serving as an essential insurance policy for productions, especially those with celebrity leads.

WATER TOWER WOODWORKERS

New York's iconic rooftop water towers are maintained by just two family-owned companies, Rosenwach Tank Company and Isseks Brothers. Together, they build and service nearly all of NYC's 17,000 wooden tanks.

These craftsmen still use 19th-century techniques, working with cedar planks and steel hoops in the same way their ancestors did. Wooden tanks remain practical for the city's older buildings because they are lighter, cheaper, and easier to maintain than steel or concrete alternatives.

SUBWAY DRUMMERS

The city's subway stations have produced their own unique musical tradition: bucket drummers. Using plastic containers and found objects, they create complex rhythms that echo through underground platforms.

While street percussion exists in many cities, New York's drummers have developed a technical style so distinctive that some have gone from subway platforms to paid performances in clubs, festivals, and even Broadway shows.

WINDOW DRESSERS

New York has elevated department store window dressing to an art form. On Fifth Avenue, window designers at Bergdorf Goodman and Saks are treated more like artists than retail workers. They create elaborate holiday displays that combine sculpture, set design, and fashion, drawing millions of visitors every year. These installations take months to design and weeks to install, becoming cultural events in their own right.

KEEPER OF THE CLOCK AT GRAND CENTRAL

Grand Central Terminal Clock. Photo via depositphotos.com

The official keeper of Grand Central Terminal's iconic Tiffany-faced clock holds one of the city's most unusual jobs. This horological expert climbs a hidden staircase weekly to maintain the $10–20 million timepiece, and synchronizes more than 100 other clocks throughout the terminal to match the national atomic clock. During Daylight Saving Time changes, adjusting every clock takes an entire night's work.

DID YOU KNOW?

Grand Central Terminal's famous clock uses Roman numerals with "IIII" instead of "IV" for the number four, a traditional style dating back centuries. Its four opal glass faces are 24 inches each, and the clock is worth far more than its nickname "the million-dollar clock" suggests.

ONLY-IN-NEW-YORK FOOD AND DRINK

UPSIDE-DOWN PIZZA

Brooklyn's L&B Spumoni Gardens serves a one-of-a-kind pizza where the cheese is placed directly on the dough, then topped with sauce. This creates a distinctive texture and sweetness that has made it a destination for pizza lovers worldwide.

WORLD'S LARGEST COLLECTION OF PIZZA BOXES

In Brooklyn, pizza tour guide Scott Wiener owns the Guinness-certified largest pizza box collection—over 1,500 boxes from 80 countries. It's a celebration of global pizza culture, from Swedish banana curry pizza boxes to Brazilian pizza with peas.

The collection is rarely on public display, but you can join one of his legendary NYC pizza tours to hear the stories behind it.

CARVEL'S TALLEST ICE CREAM CONE

In DeWitt, Carvel created the tallest ice cream cone ever—over 9 feet high and weighing 800 pounds! Built in 2016 for the chain's 85th anniversary, it set a Guinness World Record. While you can't order a nine-foot cone, you can still visit the store where ice cream history was made.

BEEF ON WECK SANDWICH

Beef on Weck sandwich. Photo by Nickgray, CC BY-SA 2.0, via Wikimedia Commons

In Buffalo, you'll find roast beef served on a kummelweck roll— a Kaiser roll topped with caraway seeds and coarse salt—along with horseradish and au jus. This sandwich is almost impossible to find outside Western New York.

THE MYSTERIOUS EGG CREAM

Despite containing neither eggs nor cream, this beloved New York drink combines milk, chocolate syrup, and seltzer water. It can't be bottled commercially because its signature frothy head disappears within minutes, so you can only experience a true egg cream fresh at the counter.

BROOKLYN'S SECRET SODA

Manhattan Special espresso coffee soda has been produced by the same family-owned company in Williamsburg since 1895. Made with real espresso, cane sugar, and carbonated water, this old-school soda has resisted national distribution and remains mostly a New York delicacy.

ONLY-IN-NEW-YORK PHENOMENA

ICE VOLCANOES OF LAKE ERIE

In the depths of winter along Buffalo's Lake Erie shoreline, strange cone-shaped "ice volcanoes" appear. When waves crash against and beneath ice shelves, pressurized water shoots upward through holes, creating icy mounds that look like miniature volcanoes. These rare natural formations draw curious onlookers every year.

FLEET WEEK: SAILORS IN THE CITY

Every May, New York hosts Fleet Week, when Navy, Marine Corps, and Coast Guard ships dock in Manhattan. Visitors can tour the ships, watch demonstrations, and see helicopters and fighter jets up close. The streets of Times Square and the subways fill with sailors in crisp uniforms, creating an iconic New York moment that mixes patriotism with the city's nonstop energy.

DID YOU KNOW?

In 2012, for the War of 1812 bicentennial, New York hosted an international parade of tall ships and naval vessels, drawing millions of spectators.

TINY MUSEUM, BIG IDEAS

Museum interior. Photo by Alexkalman, CC BY-SA 4.0, via Wikimedia Commons

Mmuseumm in Tribeca is just 36 square feet, located inside a former freight elevator. It displays overlooked, everyday objects such as prison-made items, knockoffs, and immigrant keepsakes, allowing only three visitors at a time.

ALTERNATE SIDE PARKING BALLET

New Yorkers perform a synchronized parking ritual when street cleaning rules require cars to move. During designated time windows, often about an hour or more, drivers must vacate one side of the street entirely. Many wait in their vehicles nearby until the cleaning period officially ends before reclaiming their spots.

Timing matters. You can be ticketed the moment the posted window begins or even a few minutes before it ends, regardless of when the street sweeper actually passes. Radio stations and apps track suspensions for holidays, but on regular days, it is a carefully choreographed dance between drivers and traffic enforcement.

SHAKESPEARE IN THE ASPHALT

Since 1995, free Shakespeare performances have been staged in an active Lower East Side parking lot. Actors perform between parked cars using chalk to outline their stage, improvising when vehicles enter or leave mid-performance.

CITY HALL SUBWAY STATION

The original 1904 City Hall subway station remains intact beneath Manhattan, with elegant arched ceilings, leaded skylights, and colored tilework. Though closed since 1945, you can glimpse it by staying on the downtown 6 train after its last stop.

THE TUGBOAT ROUNDUP

Each September in the Capital Region, the small town of Waterford hosts the Tugboat Roundup. Dozens of tugboats parade up the Erie Canal, sounding their horns in unison. Visitors can board the boats, learn about their history, and watch nighttime fireworks reflected in the canal waters.

WILD ANIMAL PARK CAMELS

Near Syracuse, The Wild Animal Park in Chittenango has camels that sometimes appear in parades or near rural roads. Spotting camels wandering the countryside is an amusingly unexpected sight in upstate New York.

ONLY-IN-NEW-YORK LOCATIONS

THE SMALLEST PROPERTY IN NYC

The Hess Triangle in Greenwich Village is the smallest piece of private property in New York City. Measuring just 27.5 inches (about 70 cm) per side, this tiny mosaic-tiled triangle was left behind when the city took land for street widening. The Hess family refused to give it up, and a defiant marker remains: "Property of the Hess Estate Which Has Never Been Dedicated for Public Purposes." It's still privately owned today.

MANHATTAN'S LOST TIME CAPSULE MANSION

Until its demolition in 1952, the Wendel Mansion on Fifth Avenue stood frozen in time. The eccentric Wendel sisters, its last residents, refused to install electricity, telephones, or plumbing—living by candlelight in 19th-century clothing while modern skyscrapers rose around them. Today, the building is gone, but its story lives on as a quirky chapter in New York history.

ADIRONDACK FIRE TOWERS

Scattered throughout the Adirondacks are historic fire towers that once served as lookout points for forest rangers. Today, many have been restored as hiking destinations. On a clear day, you can see into Vermont, New Hampshire, Massachusetts, Connecticut, and even Québec, Canada—a breathtaking view unique to New York's northern mountains.

THE WILD CENTER'S WILD WALK

In the Adirondacks, you can stroll among the treetops on a suspended trail 40 feet (about 12 m) above the forest floor. Highlights include a giant spiderweb net where you can lounge, a life-sized bald eagle's nest replica, and a massive bouncing net "trampoline." It's equal parts science museum and forest playground.

LUCILLE BALL-DESI ARNAZ MUSEUM

In Jamestown, Lucy's hometown, you can tour two connected museums celebrating I Love Lucy. One has costumes and memorabilia, while the other recreates classic sets from the show. Time your visit for the annual Comedy Festival each August, when top comedians perform in honor of America's favorite redhead.

PNEUMATIC POSTAL SYSTEM

From 1897–1953, New York had an underground network of pneumatic tubes that shot cylindrical containers between post offices at speeds of 30–35 mph (48–56 km/h).

Each container could carry up to 600 letters, and at its peak, the system moved 95,000 pieces of mail a day—cutting delivery times across Manhattan and Brooklyn to just minutes.

DID YOU KNOW?

Even today, pneumatic tube systems are alive and well in New York. Many hospitals use them to move medicines, lab samples, and paperwork between departments.

And at the massive B&H Photo Video store in Manhattan, purchases are whisked to cashiers through an overhead conveyor and tube system, giving customers a modern glimpse of the city's long history of underground delivery networks.

24

WAYS TO SEE AND
EXPLORE NEW YORK STATE

New York State is massive and full of variety—from the bright lights of NYC to the quiet wilderness of the Adirondacks. There are hundreds of ways to explore it, but here are the most unique ways to see the Empire State beyond the usual guidebook suggestions.

NEW YORK'S TOURISM POWERHOUSE

TOURISM IN BIG NUMBERS
New York State attracts nearly 300 million visitors annually, generating over $70 billion in economic impact and supporting almost 830,000 jobs. NYC is the top U.S. destination for international travelers, while upstate regions thrive on seasonal tourism—from lake vacations in summer to skiing in winter.

INTERNATIONAL VISITOR MAGNET
Visitors from more than 200 countries flock to NYC each year. The United Kingdom, Canada, Brazil, China, and France send the most people each year. About 20% of all overseas travelers to the U.S. include New York on their itinerary.

SEASONAL SHIFTS
NYC tourism stays steady year-round, peaking during the December holidays. Upstate, the patterns are dramatic—

summer dominates in the Finger Lakes, while the Catskills see dual peaks in summer and winter.

NEW YORK BY TRAIN

THE EMPIRE SERVICE

Amtrak's Empire Service runs from New York City to Niagara Falls, tracing the historic Hudson River and Erie Canal corridor. This scenic journey reveals the Hudson Highlands, Catskill Mountains, and charming upstate cities like Albany and Utica.

THE ADIRONDACK ROUTE

Regularly ranked among the world's most beautiful train journeys, Amtrak's Adirondack route travels from NYC to Montreal. It hugs the eastern shore of Lake Champlain with breathtaking views of the Adirondack and Green Mountains, especially stunning in fall.

HISTORIC RAILROAD RIDES

The Arcade & Attica Railroad in Western New York and the Cooperstown & Charlotte Valley Railroad in Central New York both offer nostalgic trips on vintage railcars. You'll ride through quiet farmland and river valleys while learning about the state's rich railroad history.

TIPS FOR TRAIN TRAVELERS

- Sit on the left side heading north on the Adirondack route for the best Hudson River views.

- Fall foliage season trains often sell out months ahead—book early.
- Bring binoculars for eagle spotting along the Hudson.

NEW YORK BY BOAT

EXPLORING THE ERIE CANAL

The 363-mile Erie Canal changed America's history and can still be explored today by kayak, rental boat, or guided cruise. Passing through 35 historic locks, you'll see how 19th-century engineering opened the gateway to the west.

THOUSAND ISLANDS CRUISING

At the St. Lawrence River's meeting point with Lake Ontario, the Thousand Islands region has 1,864 islands—some with castles, others barely large enough for a single tree. Cruises from Alexandria Bay let you visit the storybook Boldt Castle and hear tales of island legends.

HUDSON RIVER CRUISES

From New York Harbor up through the Hudson Valley, boat tours reveal grand estates, historic lighthouses, and stunning Palisades cliffs. In autumn, fall foliage cruises are a spectacular way to experience the river's blazing colors.

LAKE GEORGE STEAMBOATS

Lake George's Minne-Ha-Ha is one of the last operating steam paddlewheelers in America. Narrated cruises share Revolutionary War stories, local legends, and views of the Adirondack peaks surrounding the "Queen of American Lakes."

TIPS FOR BOAT TRAVELERS

- Summer and fall are the best seasons for canal cruises.
- Reserve Thousand Islands castle tours early—they sell out fast.
- Always bring an extra layer; it's cooler on the water than on land.

NEW YORK BY ROAD

ADIRONDACK NORTHWAY

Interstate 87 from Albany to the Canadian border offers jaw-dropping mountain scenery. Pull off at Lake George, Schroon Lake, or Lake Placid for classic Adirondack adventures.

SEAWAY TRAIL

This 518-mile scenic byway follows the Lake Erie, Niagara River, and Lake Ontario shorelines. It's packed with light-houses, wineries, and views of the mighty Niagara Gorge.

ROUTE 20 SCENIC BYWAY

Historic Route 20 connects charming small towns and farm-land from Sharon Springs to Lafayette. Cooperstown, with its Baseball Hall of Fame, is one of the highlights.

HAWKS NEST HIGHWAY

Route 97 winds dramatically above the Delaware River with hairpin turns and cinematic overlooks. It's so scenic it has starred in countless car commercials.

TACONIC STATE PARKWAY

This winding parkway through the Hudson Valley was designed as a scenic experience with sweeping views of farmland and forested hills. It's especially gorgeous during peak fall foliage.

TIPS FOR ROAD TRAVELERS

- Take your time on Route 20 to explore hidden gems along the way.
- Midweek drives mean fewer crowds on scenic routes.
- Visit in autumn for postcard-worthy foliage views.

NEW YORK BY AIR

SEAPLANE TOURS IN THE ADIRONDACKS

Floatplanes lift off from remote Adirondack lakes, offering unparalleled views of untouched wilderness that can't be reached by car.

MANHATTAN HELICOPTER RIDES

Soar above the Statue of Liberty, Empire State Building, or Brooklyn Bridge for a completely new perspective on NYC's skyline.

FINGER LAKES SOARING

Silent gliders at Harris Hill near Elmira ride thermal currents over vineyard-covered hills and deep blue lakes. It's one of the best gliding spots in North America.

BALLOON FESTIVALS AND RIDES

The Adirondack Balloon Festival, and rides over the Hudson Valley or Finger Lakes let you float gently over the landscape in a kaleidoscope of color.

NEW YORK BY FOOT

EMPIRE STATE TRAIL

This 750-mile trail network connects NYC, Albany, Buffalo, and the Canadian border, linking city streets with scenic greenways.

APPALACHIAN TRAIL

New York's 90-mile stretch of the Appalachian Trail winds through the Hudson Valley, including the Bear Mountain Bridge crossing—the lowest elevation on the entire trail.

FINGER LAKES GORGE TRAILS

Walk past waterfalls and ancient rock formations at Watkins Glen, Buttermilk Falls, and Taughannock Falls State Parks.

ADIRONDACK HIGH PEAKS

Hiking the Adirondack High Peaks is a rite of passage. Climbing Mount Marcy, New York's highest mountain, rewards you with sweeping wilderness views.

MUST-SEE DESTINATIONS

NIAGARA FALLS

America's oldest state park and the "Honeymoon Capital of the World," Niagara Falls straddles the U.S.–Canada border with three waterfalls: the American Falls, Bridal Veil Falls, and Horseshoe Falls. You can stand at the brink on the U.S. side or get sweeping panoramas from Canada.

LAKE GEORGE

Known as the "Queen of American Lakes," Lake George is a pristine mountain lake surrounded by Adirondack peaks. It's a hub for boating, history, and Gilded Age resorts.

THOUSAND ISLANDS

This region has over 1,800 islands dotted with castles, lighthouses, and quirky legends. It's also home to the original Thousand Island salad dressing!

COOPERSTOWN

This charming village is home to the Baseball Hall of Fame, the Fenimore Art Museum, and a dose of pure Americana.

LAKE PLACID

A two-time Winter Olympic host, Lake Placid combines Olympic history with jaw-dropping Adirondack scenery and outdoor adventures year-round.

SEASONAL ADVENTURES

SUMMER ON THE COAST

The Hamptons and Montauk on Long Island attract beachgoers, surfers, and celebrity-watchers to pristine Atlantic beaches and chic coastal towns.

FALL FOLIAGE ROAD TRIPS

From mid-September in the Adirondacks to late October in NYC, you can "chase the colors" southward for nearly six weeks. Leaf-peeping drives through the Catskills and Hudson Valley are some of the best in the Northeast.

WINTER IN THE MOUNTAINS

Lake Placid's Olympic slopes, the Catskills, and dozens of small-town ski hills turn New York into a snowy playground for skiing, snowshoeing, and ice festivals.

SPRING BLOOMS

Rochester's Lilac Festival boasts the largest lilac collection in North America, while Albany's Tulip Festival fills Washington Park with color to honor the city's Dutch heritage.

NIAGARA FALLS: AMERICA'S FIRST TOURIST ATTRACTION

THE ORIGINAL HONEYMOON CAPITAL

Niagara Falls earned the title "Honeymoon Capital of the World" after high-profile newlywed visits in the 1800s. Today, about 50,000 honeymooners still visit each year.

A SHARED WONDER

Niagara Falls sits on the U.S.–Canada border with three water-falls. Canada's side offers sweeping panoramas, while the U.S. side lets you stand right at the brink of the rushing water. Both nations jointly manage the falls for tourism and hydropower.

MAID OF THE MIST MARVEL

The Maid of the Mist boat tour started in 1846 as a ferry and now takes millions of poncho-clad visitors up close to the thundering Horseshoe Falls every year.

ILLUMINATION TRADITION

Nightly LED light shows bathe the falls in 16 million colors. The tradition began in 1860 with simple colored lights for a royal visit.

POWER PRODUCTION GIANT

Niagara's hydroelectric plants generate enough electricity to power roughly one out of every four homes across New York State and Ontario combined.

25

NEW YORK'S MYTHS, MYSTERIES, & SUPERSTITIONS

The Empire State is packed with eerie tales, ancient legends, and spine-tingling stories passed down through generations. Some are rooted in Native American folklore, while others come from early colonial ghost stories. Many are just plain unexplainable.

THE LEGEND OF SLEEPY HOLLOW

Washington Irving's classic 1819 tale of the Headless Horseman made Sleepy Hollow world-famous—though the town didn't officially adopt the spooky name until 1996!

Inspired by real Revolutionary War history and the Old Dutch Church, the story still draws thousands of visitors every Halloween. Today, you can retrace Ichabod Crane's steps and maybe glimpse a ghostly Hessian rider in the autumn mist.

CHAMP: NEW YORK'S LAKE MONSTER

Move over, Nessie—Lake Champlain has its own legendary creature! "Champ" was reportedly first spotted in 1609 by explorer Samuel de Champlain, who described a giant armored "fish." Scientists suspect it was a sturgeon, but the legend stuck. In fact, both New York and Vermont passed laws in 1981 protecting Champ, making it one of America's only legally protected cryptids.

THE CARDIFF GIANT HOAX

In 1869, workers unearthed a 10-foot "petrified man" in Cardiff, NY, near Syracuse. Some called it proof of ancient giants. In reality, it was a prank by George Hull, carved from gypsum and secretly buried. Even after Hull confessed, many refused to believe it was fake. P.T. Barnum even made his own replica, prompting Hull to complain that "Barnum's fake was stealing from my fake!"

SENECA GUNS: BOOMS FROM THE DEEP

Around the Finger Lakes, locals report mysterious booming sounds called "Seneca Guns." The earth-shaking blasts seem to come from nowhere, with no single explanation. Scientists suggest micro-earthquakes or underground gas releases, but similar unexplained booms have been heard around the world. In New York, they remain one of the state's strangest natural mysteries.

THE MAID OF THE MIST LEGEND

Niagara Falls' famous Maid of the Mist tour boats take their name from a Haudenosaunee legend. A young woman named Lelawala was sent over the Falls as a sacrifice, but instead of perishing, she was rescued by Hinum, the Thunder God. He revealed a giant serpent poisoning her people's water, and she returned with the knowledge to defeat it.

LILY DALE: VILLAGE OF SPIRITS

In western New York, Lily Dale is one of America's oldest Spiritualist communities. Founded in 1879, it's home to mediums who believe they can speak with the dead. Each summer, thousands visit for readings, healing ceremonies, and quiet walks to Inspiration Stump—where spirits are said to pass messages to the living.

BANNERMAN'S CASTLE: ARSENAL OF GHOSTS

Bannerman's Castle. Photo by depositphotos.com

Perched on a Hudson River island, Bannerman's Castle was built by a military surplus dealer to store weapons—and it literally blew up in 1920 when tons of munitions ignited. After a later fire and decades of decay, the ruins became a ghost-hunter's dream. Visitors report phantom lights, eerie whispers, and the ghostly figure of a woman in white.

THE DUNDERBERG GOBLIN

Early Dutch settlers warned of a mischievous goblin haunting Dunderberg Mountain along the Hudson River. He was said to stir up sudden storms to punish disrespectful sailors, appearing as a little man in old Dutch clothes and a sugarloaf hat. Modern meteorologists say the mountain's shape causes odd weather—but some old-timers still tip their hats when passing, just in case.

THE GHOST SHIP OF THE HUDSON

Legend says a phantom Dutch ship sails the Hudson River before disasters. Some connect it to Henry Hudson, whose mutinous crew abandoned him in 1611. While no sightings were officially recorded before big events like the Great Fire of 1835, foggy mornings still inspire tales from fishermen who swear they've seen a schooner vanish into the mist.

THE MONTAUK PROJECT

On Long Island's far eastern tip, Camp Hero Air Force Station fuels conspiracy theories about secret government experiments. Stories of time travel, mind control, and even alien contact began with a 1992 book and inspired the TV show Stranger Things. Officially, it was just a Cold War radar base—but its eerie radar tower and empty bunkers still attract curious visitors.

THE SCREAMING TUNNEL OF NIAGARA

Step into this dark limestone tunnel near Niagara Falls at midnight, light a match, and it's said to blow out just before you hear a girl's scream. Some say she died in a fire, others claim she was murdered. The wind-tunnel effect might explain the blown-out match, but the mysterious scream? That's still up for debate.

WASHINGTON SQUARE PARK'S FORGOTTEN DEAD

Beneath Manhattan's lively Washington Square Park lie over 20,000 bodies—paupers, prisoners, and yellow fever victims buried there when it was a potter's field from 1797 to 1825. During park renovations in 2015, workers unearthed more human remains. Today, visitors report cold spots, whispers, and children playing with invisible friends in old-fashioned clothes.

LAKE RONKONKOMA'S VENGEFUL PRINCESS

Long Island's deepest lake has a dark reputation. Legend says it claims one man every year, lured by the ghost of a Native princess who drowned herself after forbidden love. The lake's sudden drop-offs and swirling currents make it dangerous—especially for men—which keeps the eerie legend alive.

THE WENDIGO OF THE ADIRONDACKS

Deep in the Adirondacks lurks the Wendigo—a spirit from Algonquin folklore said to possess those who resort to cannibalism in harsh winters. Early settlers told chilling stories of "Wendigo psychosis," where people were consumed by hunger for human flesh. Today, the Wendigo remains a haunting symbol of greed, survival, and nature's unforgiving power.

THE GHOSTS OF ELLIS ISLAND

More than 12 million immigrants passed through Ellis Island between 1892 and 1954, but thousands died waiting for entry into America. The abandoned hospital buildings are said to echo with their spirits. Security guards and visitors report phantom footsteps, whispers in many languages, and sudden cold spots. Haunted or not, Ellis Island carries an unforgettable emotional weight.

THE LADY IN WHITE OF DURAND EASTMAN PARK

In Rochester's Durand Eastman Park, a ghostly woman in white roams the lakefront with two phantom dogs, searching for her missing daughter. Locals say she died of heartbreak in the 1800s. Foggy mornings bring sightings of her misty figure, a story so haunting it inspired the 1988 film Lady in White.

THE HAUNTED SPLIT ROCK QUARRY

Just outside Syracuse lies Split Rock Quarry, the site of a 1918 munitions factory explosion that killed 50 workers. The blast was so powerful it was felt 30 miles away. Today, rusted ruins remain, and visitors report glowing orbs, phantom screams, and the distant sound of machinery that no longer exists.

DID YOU KNOW?

New York has so many ghost stories that it's often called one of America's most haunted states. In fact, more than 1,000 locations in New York are listed in ghost hunter guides and paranormal registries. From haunted theaters on Broadway to eerie mountain trails in the Adirondacks, there's a legend lurking in almost every county—making the Empire State a supernatural hotspot for thrill seekers.

26

LEARN TO SPEAK NEW YORK

Welcome to the Empire State, where the way people talk is as diverse as the landscape. In Manhattan, conversations move as fast as the subway, while upstate, words stretch out with a more relaxed rhythm. From slang that confuses visitors to food terms you won't hear anywhere else, New York's vocabulary reflects its mix of cultures, history, and attitude.

NEW YORK CITY SLANG & EVERYDAY EXPRESSIONS

BODEGA

A neighborhood cornerstone, the bodega is a small corner store selling everything from sandwiches and coffee to cat food and toilet paper. Many are family-run and known for their resident bodega cat lounging on the counter. "I'm stopping at the bodega for a bacon-egg-and-cheese and a coffee."

REGULAR COFFEE

In New York City, a "regular coffee" isn't black—it comes with milk and sugar already added, usually about two packets of sugar and a splash of milk or cream. Order just "coffee" at a deli or bodega and this sweet, creamy version will almost always be what you get. Anywhere else, a "regular" coffee might mean plain or black—but in NYC, it definitely does not.

BRICK

When the temperature is brutally cold, New Yorkers say "It's brick outside." It's the kind of cold that cuts through your coat and makes your face numb. "Bundle up—it's brick out there today!"

DEADASS

A serious New Yorker intensifier meaning "seriously" or "for real." It's used to emphasize honesty or certainty. "I'm deadass telling you—that was the best slice of pizza I've ever had."

ON LINE

While most Americans stand in line, New Yorkers stand on line when they're waiting. "I was on line at the DMV for three hours!"

STOOP

The front steps of a brownstone or townhouse, often a social gathering spot in summer. Kids play stoop ball, neighbors sit and chat, and friends meet "on the stoop."

SCHLEP

Borrowed from Yiddish, meaning to carry or drag something with effort—or to describe a long, inconvenient trip. "I had to schlep these groceries six blocks because I couldn't get a cab."

MAD

Used as an intensifier meaning "very" or "a lot of." "There were mad people at the Yankees game last night."

TIGHT

Depending on context, it can mean "angry" or "close friends."

"He got tight when I was late" vs. "We're tight—we grew up together."

FUHGEDDABOUDIT

The classic New York phrase that can mean forget it, that's impossible, that's amazing, or absolutely not. It all depends on tone. "You want to find parking in Manhattan on a Friday night? Fuhgeddaboudit."

The phrase is so iconic that it has even appeared on official highway signs. Electronic boards have flashed messages like "Leaving Brooklyn? Fuhgeddaboudit!" giving drivers one last dose of borough attitude before they cross the bridge.

YOU GOOD?

A multi-purpose phrase that can mean "Are you okay?", "Do you need anything else?", or "Are we all set?" Context is everything. "Here's your coffee. You good?"

ON GOD

Used to emphasize honesty, like saying I swear. "On God, that was the best bagel I've ever had."

SAY LESS

Means I understand completely or you don't need to explain further. "You need help moving this weekend? Say less—I'll be there."

NOT FOR NOTHING

A phrase that softens the blow of an opinion, especially one that might be unpopular. "Not for nothing, but the Yankees are making the playoffs this year."

HOW YOU DOIN'?

A casual greeting (made famous by Joey on Friends) that doesn't actually expect an answer. Said with a distinctive rising intonation: "Hey, how you doin'?"

SUBWAY & TRANSIT TALK

UPTOWN & DOWNTOWN

In Manhattan, directions are simple: uptown is north, downtown is south. These terms apply to both locations and subway directions. "Take the uptown 6 train to 86th Street" means you're heading north.

SHOWTIME!

When someone announces "It's showtime!" on the subway, brace yourself for an impromptu dance routine. Performers flip, spin, or hang in amazing feats of athletic ability from the poles —tourists cheer, but seasoned commuters usually just sigh or ignore the performance.

ON THE PLATFORM

Waiting for a subway train. "I was on the platform for 20 minutes before they even announced the delay."

EXPRESS VS. LOCAL

Express trains skip stops, cutting travel time in half if you know where to catch them. Locals stop at every station. A true New Yorker knows when to switch between the two types of train ride to shave minutes off a commute.

METROCARD SWIPE

For decades, getting your MetroCard swipe just right was an unspoken New York skill. Hesitate too long and you'd get the dreaded "Swipe Again." Tourists were instantly spotted by their failed attempts at the turnstile.

Today, the MTA is replacing MetroCards with OMNY, a tap-and-go system that works with contactless cards, smartphones, or dedicated OMNY cards. The iconic swipe may be fading into history, but longtime New Yorkers still remember mastering the motion.

THE BQE

Short for the Brooklyn-Queens Expressway. It's infamous for constant traffic jams and construction. "Avoid the BQE at rush hour unless you want to sit still for an hour."

THE JACKIE

What locals call the Jackie Robinson Parkway, a narrow and winding route through Brooklyn and Queens. Low bridges and tight curves make it tricky for large trucks. "Take the Jackie" is classic outer-borough navigation advice.

THE GEORGE

A nickname New Yorkers use for the George Washington Bridge, which connects Manhattan to New Jersey. Locals also call it "the GW." You might hear someone say, "We're taking the George to avoid tunnel traffic."

With more than 100 million vehicles crossing each year, it's one of the busiest bridges in the world.

THE TACONIC

The Taconic State Parkway is a scenic, winding highway up the Hudson Valley. It's beautiful in fall but nerve-wracking for drivers used to wide highways.

THE NORTHWAY

The local nickname for Interstate 87 north of Albany, the highway that runs toward the Adirondacks and the Canadian border. "We hit a snowstorm on the Northway coming back from Lake Placid."

South of Albany, I-87 becomes part of the New York State Thruway, but the stretch heading north has long been known simply as "the Northway."

REGIONAL FOOD TERMS

HERO

In New York City and much of Downstate New York, a long sandwich filled with meats, cheeses, and toppings is called a hero—not a sub. "I'll take an Italian hero with everything on it."

Head up to the Southern Tier, though, and you might hear the same sandwich called a hoagie, showing how New York's food vocabulary shifts from region to region.

WEDGE

Head to Westchester or the Hudson Valley and you'll find the same sandwich (a hero or sub) called a wedge. "I ordered a turkey wedge for lunch."

PIE

When New Yorkers say "pie," they're usually talking about pizza, not dessert. "Let's grab a pie from Joe's before the game."

WINGS

In Buffalo, you never say "Buffalo wings"—they're just wings, and they're served hot, medium, or mild. "We're ordering 50 hot wings for the party."

BEEF ON WECK

A Buffalo specialty: tender roast beef on a kummelweck roll topped with salt and caraway seeds, usually served with horse-radish. "Any visit to Buffalo requires a beef on weck sandwich."

SPIEDIE

From Binghamton, this dish features marinated cubes of meat (usually chicken) grilled on skewers or served in a sandwich. "We're heading to the Spiedie Fest this weekend."

GARBAGE PLATE

Rochester's famous late-night meal—macaroni salad, home fries, meat (often burgers or hot dogs), and a special sauce, all piled on one plate. "After the bar, we grabbed garbage plates at 2 AM."

SALT POTATOES

A Syracuse picnic staple—small potatoes boiled in salty water, leaving a unique crust, then drenched in melted butter. "It's not summer in Central New York without salt potatoes."

CHICKEN RIGGIES

A Utica favorite: rigatoni pasta with chicken, peppers, and a spicy tomato cream sauce. "The annual Riggie Fest draws chefs from all over."

TOMATO PIE

Different from pizza, tomato pie is thick bread topped with a sweet tomato sauce and served room temperature, especially popular in Utica and Rome. "We always grab tomato pie on the way through Utica."

LOGANBERRY

A sweet-tart, deep red drink you'll find in Western New York diners and delis. "No Buffalo picnic is complete without loganberry to drink."

REGIONAL & DIRECTIONAL TERMS

THE CITY

Even though all five boroughs are technically part of New York City, "The City" always means Manhattan. Brooklyn, Queens, the Bronx, and Staten Island residents say they're "going to the city" when heading into Manhattan.

THE ISLAND

When locals say "the Island," they mean Long Island—not Manhattan, even though it technically is an island. "My parents still live out on the Island."

UPSTATE

Ask a New Yorker what "upstate" means, and you'll get a dozen different answers. For NYC residents, it's anywhere north of the city; for people in Albany, it means areas north of them. The definition is hotly debated—and that's very New York.

DOWNSTATE

The opposite of upstate, this refers to New York City, Long Island, and the lower Hudson Valley. Someone moving from Albany to Manhattan might say they're "heading downstate."

NORTH FORK / SOUTH FORK

The two eastern peninsulas of Long Island. The South Fork includes the Hamptons (famous for luxury summer homes), while the North Fork is known for wineries and farmland.

THE NORTH COUNTRY

The region encompassing the Adirondacks and the St. Lawrence River Valley. It's rugged, remote, and beloved by skiers, hikers, and nature lovers.

THE SOUTHERN TIER

The strip of counties along the Pennsylvania border, west of the Catskills. It's more rural, with Binghamton as its largest city.

THE CAPITAL REGION

The Albany-Schenectady-Troy metro area. Locals use "Capital Region" as shorthand for this cluster of cities that revolve around New York's state capital.

CITIOT

A not-so-nice term used by upstaters for NYC visitors who don't understand rural life. It combines "city" and "idiot," usually applied to someone trying to pet a wild deer or complaining there's no Wi-Fi.

DOWNSTATER

A gentler term for someone from NYC or its immediate suburbs. You'll often hear it in small towns when describing visitors from the metro area.

WEATHER TALK

LAKE EFFECT

When cold air sweeps across the Great Lakes, it picks up moisture and dumps massive amounts of snow on nearby towns. Buffalo and Syracuse are famous for getting buried under feet of lake-effect snow while nearby areas stay clear.

SNOW BELT

The regions east of Lake Erie and Lake Ontario that get hammered year after year by heavy lake-effect snow. Syracuse, smack in the snow belt, averages over 120 inches of snow annually!

BLACK ICE SEASON

That tricky winter period when melted snow refreezes into invisible sheets of ice on roads. Drivers dread it, and seasoned locals know to take it slow. "Be careful—it's black ice season."

THE THRUWAY'S CLOSED

When Interstate 90—the main New York State Thruway—closes due to snowstorms, it's serious. Locals use it as a benchmark for just how bad the weather is. "It's so bad they closed the Thruway."

CLIPPER

A "clipper" is a quick-moving snowstorm from Canada that blows through, drops a few inches, and is gone within hours. "There's a clipper coming tonight, but it won't be too bad."

PRONUNCIATION QUIRKS

HOUSTON STREET

In Manhattan, it's pronounced HOW-stun, not like the city in Texas. Mispronouncing it as HYOO-ston instantly marks you as a tourist.

The trendy neighborhood of SoHo gets its name from being South of Houston Street.

POUGHKEEPSIE

This Hudson Valley city is puh-KIP-see, not poh-KEEP-see.

SCHENECTADY

This upstate city near Albany is skuh-NEK-tuh-dee. It's a mouthful, even for locals!

GREENE COUNTY

Despite the spelling, it's simply pronounced Green, not Green-ee.

STATEN ISLAND

Locals blend it into STAT-nin Island, skipping that middle syllable.

COFFEE

In a classic NYC accent, it becomes CAWF-ee.

LONG ISLAND

In that same accent, it almost sounds like Lawn-GUY-land.

WATER

Often pronounced WAW-tuh, with the "t" softened or disappearing altogether.

ORANGE

In NYC, it can sound more like AH-rinj than OR-inj.

FOREST HILLS

Queens locals emphasize the first syllable: FAH-rest Hills.

27

ODD NEW YORK LAWS

New York is famous for its fast pace and big-city energy—but dig into its legal code, and you'll find some surprisingly quirky rules. Some date back to the 1800s, while others were passed in the modern era to solve very specific problems. Many are rarely enforced but still on the books, offering a fascinating glimpse into New York's history and priorities.

MASKED GATHERINGS PROHIBITED (UNTIL RECENTLY)

Back in 1845, New York made it illegal for two or more people to gather in public while wearing masks. The law was created after tenant farmers wore disguises to protest high rents and attack law enforcement. It stayed in place for 175 years, resurfacing during protests, until it was finally repealed in 2020 during the COVID pandemic. Today, a new law only adds extra penalties if someone commits another crime while masked.

HANDLE YOUR HOUSE KEY WITH CARE

Under New York Penal Law, even possessing someone else's house key—or an impression of one—with the intent to commit a crime counts as having "burglar's tools." You don't even have to use it to be charged; simply carrying it for the wrong reason is enough to land you in trouble.

MANHOLE COVER PROTECTION

Opening or removing a manhole cover in New York City without authorization can result in up to a year in jail. The law exists for obvious safety reasons, but the penalty still surprises many people—no casual urban exploring here!

ADULTERY IS STILL ILLEGAL

Believe it or not, adultery is still a Class B misdemeanor in New York. Technically, it's punishable by up to 90 days in jail or a $500 fine, though it hasn't been enforced in decades. The law remains on the books as a relic of an older moral code.

FORTUNE-TELLING FOR ENTERTAINMENT ONLY

In New York, fortune-telling for money is only legal if it's clearly advertised as "for entertainment purposes." Palm readers, tarot card readers, and psychics who claim real supernatural abilities can actually face charges if they don't give this disclaimer.

SELECTIVE HONKING

Despite the constant blare of horns in NYC, it's actually illegal to honk except in an emergency. The fine for unnecessary honking can be as high as $350. Enforcement is spotty, but signs across the city still warn drivers not to do it.

NO SPITTING ON THE SIDEWALK

Spitting in public has been banned in New York City since 1896. The law was originally passed to stop the spread of tuberculosis but remains on the books today as an old-school public health regulation.

DON'T FEED THE PIGEONS

In certain public areas, especially near airports, feeding pigeons can get you fined up to $1,000. The rule is meant to reduce pigeon mess and prevent flocks of birds from interfering with airplanes.

DANCING WITHOUT A LICENSE (NOW REPEALED)

For almost a century, New Yorkers couldn't legally dance in bars or restaurants without a special "cabaret license." This Prohibition-era law was finally repealed in 2017 after decades of criticism for stifling nightlife.

THE HANGMAN'S NOOSE LAW

It's a felony in New York to place a noose in public or on someone's property with intent to threaten or harass. This 2007 law was passed in response to a rise in hate crimes, carrying up to four years in prison.

RECKLESS STUNTS ARE STILL ILLEGAL

New York has no patience for dangerous antics like throwing objects at people for fun or jumping from high buildings. While not listed as specific "weird" laws, these acts are prosecuted under reckless endangerment statutes to keep public spaces safe.

28

QUOTABLES & QUIRKY NEW YORK-ISMS

New York has inspired countless writers, artists, musicians, and dreamers. From heartfelt reflections on its energy and resilience to sharp one-liners about its quirks, the Empire State has a way of leaving an unforgettable mark on those who experience it. Here's a collection of some of the most memorable things ever said—or sung—about New York.

ICONIC QUOTES ABOUT NEW YORK & NEW YORK STATE

"London is satisfied, Paris is resigned, but New York is always hopeful. Always it believes that something good is about to come off, and it must hurry to meet it."

DOROTHY PARKER, WRITER AND CRITIC

"One belongs to New York instantly. One belongs to it as much in five minutes as in five years."

THOMAS WOLFE, NOVELIST

"One can't paint New York as it is, but rather as it is felt."

GEORGIA O'KEEFFE, ARTIST

"My favorite thing about New York is the people, because I think they're misunderstood. I don't think people realize how kind New York people are."

BILL MURRAY, ACTOR AND COMEDIAN

"If London is a watercolor, New York is an oil painting."

PETER SHAFFER, PLAYWRIGHT

"Once you have lived in New York and it has become your home, no place else is good enough."

JOHN STEINBECK, AUTHOR

"Cities have the capability of providing something for everybody, only because, and only when, they are created by everybody."

JANE JACOBS, URBAN THEORIST

"The true New Yorker secretly believes that people living anywhere else have to be, in some sense, kidding."

JOHN UPDIKE, NOVELIST

"Upstate New York in the middle of October. You can't get more beautiful than that."

PAUL REISER, ACTOR AND COMEDIAN

POP CULTURE QUOTES & LYRICS

New York has been immortalized in films, TV, and music—sometimes romanticized, sometimes teased, but always larger than life.

MUSIC

"Start spreadin' the news, I'm leaving today / I want to be a part of it—New York, New York."

FRANK SINATRA, (THEME FROM NEW YORK, NEW YORK, 1977)

"I'm in a New York state of mind."

BILLY JOEL, (NEW YORK STATE OF MIND, 1976)

"In New York, concrete jungle where dreams are made of / There's nothin' you can't do."

JAY-Z & ALICIA KEYS, (EMPIRE STATE OF MIND, 2009)

"The lights are so bright but they never blind me."

TAYLOR SWIFT, (WELCOME TO NEW YORK, 2014)

"No sleep till Brooklyn!"

BEASTIE BOYS, (NO SLEEP TILL BROOKLYN, 1986)

MOVIES & TV SHOWS

Sex and the City – "If you can only have one great love, then New York may just be mine."

CARRIE BRADSHAW (PLAYED BY SARAH JESSICA PARKER)

Spider-Man (2002) "You mess with one of us, you mess with all of us!"

NEW YORKERS ON THE BRIDGE

Ghostbusters (1984) – "We came, we saw, we kicked its ass!"

DR. PETER VENKMAN (PLAYED BY BILL MURRAY)

29

QUIZ YOURSELF

1. What percentage of New York State residents are either immigrants or children of immigrants?

    A. 20%
    B. 30%
    C. 40%
    D. 50%

2. In New York City, what does ordering a "regular coffee" usually get you?

    A. Black coffee
    B. Coffee with cream only
    C. Coffee with about two packets of sugar and milk
    D. Espresso with foam

3. Which New York village hosted the Winter Olympics twice?

    A. Saratoga Springs
    B. Lake George
    C. Lake Placid
    D. Cooperstown

4. New York State produces more maple syrup than any other state in the U.S.

    A. True
    B. False

5. What was "Charg-It," created in Brooklyn in 1946?

    A. The first debit card
    B. A subway fare card
    C. A local bank-issued charge card
    D. A wartime ration system

6. Egg creams, despite their name, contain neither eggs nor cream.

    A. True
    B. False

7. New York bagels are boiled before they are baked.

    A. True
    B. False

8. Which New York waterway is technically a fjord, carved by glaciers during the last Ice Age?

    A. Erie Canal
    B. Hudson River
    C. Niagara River
    D. St. Lawrence River

9. The Garbage Plate is a famous culinary creation from which New York city?

    A. Albany
    B. Syracuse
    C. Buffalo
    D. Rochester

10. What is New York's official state beverage?

    A. Apple cider
    B. Milk
    C. Wine
    D. Manhattan cocktail

11. The iconic "I ♥ NY" logo was designed during a taxi ride and the designer charged $200,000 for it.

    A. True
    B. False

12. New York State has an official state sport, which is baseball.

    A. True
    B. False

13. Times Square billboards synchronize every night at midnight to display contemporary art in what's called the "Midnight Moment."

    A. True
    B. False

14. Which famous hotel invented room service, the Waldorf salad, and Eggs Benedict?

    A. The Plaza
    B. Waldorf Astoria
    C. St. Regis
    D. Roosevelt Hotel

15. What does the term "the Oblong" refer to?

    A. A mountain range
    B. A river valley
    C. A historic border agreement with Connecticut
    D. A subway line

16. How many pieces did the Statue of Liberty arrive in?

    A. 50
    B. 151
    C. 350
    D. 1,000

17. Why were funeral trains used in early New York history?

    A. To save money on burial costs
    B. To transport the dead to cemeteries outside
    Manhattan
    C. To honor military veterans
    D. To avoid street traffic

18. The Nike missile program is named after the shoe company.

    A. True
    B. False

19. The New York Yankees have won 27 World Series championships, making them the most successful franchise in professional sports history.

    A. True
    B. False

20. What hidden feature was added to Grand Central Terminal's ceiling during its 1990s restoration?

    A. A time capsule
    B. A painting of a whale
    C. A telescope
    D. A secret apartment

30

QUIZ ANSWERS

1. What percentage of New York State residents are either immigrants or children of immigrants?

    A. 20%
    B. 30%
    C. 40%
    D. 50%

2. In New York City, what does ordering a "regular coffee" usually get you?

    A. Black coffee
    B. Coffee with cream only
    C. Coffee with about two packets of sugar and milk
    D. Espresso with foam

3. Which New York village hosted the Winter Olympics twice?

    A. Saratoga Springs
    B. Lake George
    C. Lake Placid
    D. Cooperstown

4. New York State produces more maple syrup than any other state in the U.S.

> A. True
> **B. False** (Vermont is the number one producer of maple syrup in the U.S.)

5. What was "Charg-It," created in Brooklyn in 1946?

> A. The first debit card
> B. A subway fare card
> **C. A local bank-issued charge card**
> D. A wartime ration system

6. Egg creams, despite their name, contain neither eggs nor cream.

> **A. True**
> B. False

7. New York bagels are boiled before they are baked.

> **A. True**
> B. False

8. Which New York waterway is technically a fjord, carved by glaciers during the last Ice Age?

> A. Erie Canal
> **B. Hudson River**
> C. Niagara River
> D. St. Lawrence River

9. The Garbage Plate is a famous culinary creation from which New York city?

    A. Albany
    B. Syracuse
    C. Buffalo
    D. Rochester

10. What is New York's official state beverage?

    A. Apple cider
    B. Milk
    C. Wine
    D. Manhattan cocktail

11. The iconic "I ♥ NY" logo was designed during a taxi ride and the designer charged $200,000 for it.

    A. True
    B. False (He doodled the design in red crayon on the back of an envelope in a taxi in 1976 and donated it to the state's tourism campaign, never charging a fee.)

12. New York State has an official state sport, which is baseball.

    A. True
    B. False (New York State doesn't have an official state sport)

13. Times Square billboards synchronize every night at midnight to display contemporary art in what's called the "Midnight Moment."

A. True
B. False

14. Which famous hotel invented room service, the Waldorf salad, and Eggs Benedict?

A. The Plaza
B. Waldorf Astoria
C. St. Regis
D. Roosevelt Hotel

15. What does the term "the Oblong" refer to?

A. A mountain range
B. A river valley
C. A historic border agreement with Connecticut
D. A subway line

16. How many pieces did the Statue of Liberty arrive in?

A. 50
B. 151
C. 350
D. 1,000

17. Why were funeral trains used in early New York history?

A. To save money on burial costs
B. To transport the dead to cemeteries outside Manhattan
C. To honor military veterans
D. To avoid street traffic

18. The Nike missile program is named after the shoe company.

A. True
B. False (It's named after the Greek goddess of victory.)

19. The New York Yankees have won 27 World Series championships, making them the most successful franchise in professional sports history.

A. True
B. False

20. What hidden feature was added to Grand Central Terminal's ceiling during its 1990s restoration?

A. A time capsule
B. A painting of a whale
C. A telescope
D. A secret apartment

ACKNOWLEDGMENTS

Creating this book has been a wonderful journey. New York is a state bursting with history, culture, innovation, and personality, and the deeper I researched, the more fascinating stories I discovered. From towering skyscrapers and world-changing inventions to quirky traditions and hidden gems, the Empire State never stops surprising.

I'm also deeply grateful to Joe Levit , whose thoughtful editing and sharp eye for detail helped strengthen this manuscript. Your suggestions and insights made the book clearer, stronger, and more enjoyable to read.

To my talented cover designer, Paul Hawkins, who has brought the entire *Amazing States of America* series to life visually—thank you for once again capturing the spirit of this book so beautifully.

A huge thank you as well to Hank Musolf, my dedicated fact checker. With a book filled with hundreds of facts, your careful research and attention to detail helped ensure that every nugget of information is as accurate as possible.

To my fantastic beta readers, Anna Jones, William Harang, Alicia Kozak, Shari Zedeck, Alan Guyana, Galiah Morgenstern, Craig Jones, Linnie Skidmore, Leslie Kammerer, Peter Alexiev, Rose Scott, Lisa Deasy and Lorraine Donlin, who eagerly read early drafts and offered thoughtful feedback—your questions, suggestions, and enthusiasm helped shape this book into its best form.

And finally, thank you to you—the reader. Whether you're a lifelong New Yorker, a visitor who fell in love with the state, or simply someone who enjoys discovering fascinating facts, your curiosity is the reason books like this exist. I hope these pages help you see New York in a new light and inspire you to keep exploring the stories that make this state so extraordinary.

LEARN SOMETHING?
PLEASE LEAVE A REVIEW

If you learned something new or enjoyed these fun facts about New York, I'd truly appreciate it if you shared your thoughts in a review.

Even a short review helps other curious readers discover the book—and your feedback means a lot to me as an author.

Scan the QR code below to find the best place to leave a review based on where you purchased the book.

https://tinyurl.com/KNB-leave-a-review

Not sure what to write? You could mention things like:

- Your favorite fun fact from the book
- Something new you learned about New York
- Who you think would enjoy this book

Thank you for taking a moment to share your feedback—it truly helps independent authors like me!

DON'T FORGET YOUR BONUS

As a **special bonus** and as a **thank you** for purchasing this book, I created a **FREE New York companion quiz e-book** with **over 100 fun questions and answers** taken from this book.

Get the FREE bonus quiz e-book here:
https://tinyurl.com/nyquizbook-bonus

Test your knowledge of New York and quiz your friends.
Enjoy!

ABOUT THE AUTHOR

Marianne Jennings is a self-proclaimed adventure craver with a lifelong love of learning, exploring, and asking "Wait—really?"

An American living in the United Kingdom, she spends a lot of time noticing cultural quirks, everyday habits, and the small details that make places feel unique.

Through her books, Marianne enjoys sharing fascinating, surprising, and often overlooked facts about places, people, and cultures, turning everyday knowledge into something entertaining and easy to remember.

Marianne also writes *An American's Guide to British Life* on Substack, where she explores the humorous, confusing, and delightful similarities and differences between life in the U.S. and the U.K.

Find more of her books at KnowledgeNuggetBooks.com and follow her along on Substack at:

 anamericansguidetobritishlife.substack.com

ALSO BY MARIANNE JENNINGS

 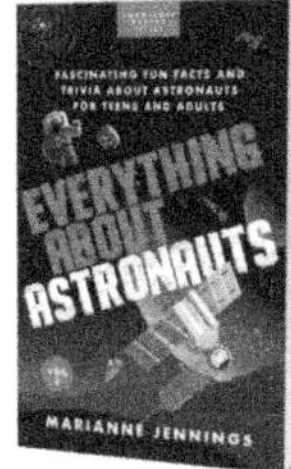 

So You Think You Know CANADA, Eh? (2nd Edition)

Amazing Tennessee!

Amazing Alaska!

Everything About Astronauts Vol 1 & 2

Quirky Careers & Offbeat Occupations

Christmas Fun Facts!

Made in the USA
Monee, IL
07 July 2026

56546393R00193